Georges Méliès

MANCHESTER
UNIVERSITY PRESS

DIANA HOLMES and ROBERT INGRAM *series editors*
DUDLEY ANDREW *series consultant*

Luc Besson   SUSAN HAYWARD

Claude Chabrol   GUY AUSTIN

Diane Kurys   CARRIE TARR

Coline Serreau   BRIGITTE ROLLET

François Truffaut   DIANA HOLMES AND ROBERT INGRAM

Agnès Varda   ALISON SMITH

forthcoming titles

Jean-Jacques Beineix   PHIL POWRIE

Bertrand Blier   SUE HARRIS

Robert Bresson   KEITH READER

Jean-Luc Godard   STEVE CANNON AND ELIANE MEYER

Jean Renoir   MARTIN O'SHAUGHNESSY

FRENCH FILM DIRECTORS

Georges Méliès
The birth of the *auteur*

ELIZABETH EZRA

Manchester University Press
MANCHESTER AND NEW YORK

distributed exclusively in the USA by St. Martin's Press

Copyright © Elizabeth Ezra 2000

The right of Elizabeth Ezra to be identified as the author of this work has
been asserted by her in accordance with the Copyright, Designs and Patents
Act 1988.

Published by Manchester University Press
Oxford Road, Manchester M13 9NR, UK
and Room 400, 175 Fifth Avenue, New York, NY 10010, USA
http://www.man.ac.uk/mup

Distributed exclusively in the USA by
St. Martin's Press, Inc., 175 Fifth Avenue, New York,
NY 10010, USA

Distributed exclusively in Canada by
UBC Press, University of British Columbia, 6344 Memorial Road,
Vancouver, BC, Canada V6T 1Z2

British Library Cataloguing-in-Publication Data
A catalogue record for this book is available from the British Library

Library of Congress Cataloging-in-Publication Data applied for

ISBN 0 7190 5395 1 *hardback*
     0 7190 5396 x *paperback*

First published 2000

07 06 05 04 03 02 01 00   10 9 8 7 6 5 4 3 2 1

Typeset in Scala with Meta display
by Koinonia, Manchester
Printed in Great Britain
by Bookcraft (Bath) Ltd, Midsomer Norton

Contents

List of plates

Plates 1–4, 6 and 8–11 were supplied by and are reproduced with permission from the Museum of Modern Art, New York; plates 5 and 7 were supplied by and are reproduced with permission from the Collection Roger-Viollet.

Series editors' foreword

To an anglophone audience, the combination of the words 'French' and 'cinema' evokes a particular kind of film: elegant and wordy, sexy but serious – an image as dependent on national stereotypes as is that of the crudely commercial Hollywood blockbuster, which is not to say that either image is without foundation. Over the past two decades, this generalised sense of a significant relationship between French identity and film has been explored in scholarly books and articles, and has entered the curriculum at university level and, in Britain, at A-level. The study of film as an art-form and (to a lesser extent) as industry, has become a popular and widespread element of French Studies, and French cinema has acquired an important place within Film Studies. Meanwhile, the growth in multi-screen and 'art-house' cinemas, together with the development of the video industry, has led to the greater availability of foreign-language films to an English-speaking audience. Responding to these developments, this series is designed for students and teachers seeking information and accessible but rigorous critical study of French cinema, and for the enthusiastic filmgoer who wants to know more.

The adoption of a director-based approach raises questions about *auteurism*. A series that categorises films not according to period or to genre (for example), but to the person who directed them, runs the risk of espousing a romantic view of film as the product of solitary inspiration. On this model, the critic's role might seem to be that of discovering continuities, revealing a necessary coherent set of themes and motifs which correspond to the particular genius of the individual. This is not our aim: the *auteur* perspective on film, itself most clearly articulated in France in the early 1950s, will be interrogated in certain volumes of the series, and, throughout, the director will be treated as one highly significant element in a complex process of film production and reception which includes socio-economic and political determinants, the work of a large and highly skilled team of artists and technicians, the mechanisms of production and distribution, and the complex and multiply determined responses of spectators.

The work of some of the directors in the series is already known outside France, that of others is less so – the aim is both to provide informative and original English-language studies of established figures, and to extend the range of French directors known to anglophone students of cinema. We intend the series to contribute to the promotion of the informal and formal study of French films, and to the pleasure of those who watch them.

DIANA HOLMES
ROBERT INGRAM

Acknowledgements

I wish to thank the Carnegie Trust for a grant that allowed me to travel to libraries and film archives. I am very grateful to Siân Reynolds and Peter France for kindly providing me with a place to stay in Paris while researching this book. Florianne Wild, too, allowed me to take refuge in her Parisian digs when I was in the final throes of the manuscript. And I can't thank Letizia Panizza and Joe Harris enough for giving me a home away from home in London on many a working vacation.

I will always be grateful to Dudley Andrew and Steve Ungar for convincing me that studying film isn't so bad after all. For reading and making helpful comments on the manuscript for this book I wish to thank Sue Harris, Paul Jackson and Rebecca Spang, all of whom have also offered encouragement and support. Diana Holmes and Robert Ingram have been wonderful editors, making invaluable suggestions on the first draft. I have also benefited from conversations about some of the ideas in this book with Sandy Flitterman-Lewis, Jane Sillars, Meryl Tyers and Mike Witt. (However, despite all the assistance I have received with this project, it is safe to assume that any errors in judgement are mine alone.)

Finally, I must thank the staff at the Bibliothèque du Film in Paris, which has been an oasis of helpfulness in a desert of bureaucracy.

Preface

Invaluable contributions to early film scholarship have been made by Méliès's descendants, some of whom have made important discoveries about the technical aspects of Méliès's production practices. Researchers who do not have the good fortune to be related to Méliès, however, face difficult challenges in gaining access to films and archival materials. Fortunately, many of the films Méliès made after 1902 are available on video in the United States (from FACETS video in Chicago), and there are substantial film archives in London (the National Film Archive of the British Film Institute) and the United States (the Library of Congress in Washington, D.C., the Museum of Modern Art in New York City and the George Eastman House in Rochester, New York). A selection of fifteen beautifully restored films was broadcast on the ARTE satellite television channel in German and French on 23 December 1997 and a VHS version of this three-hour programme, which also includes an excellent biography, is available in France under the title *Méliès le cinémagicien*. Finally, the user-friendly Bibliothèque du Film (BiFi) in Paris houses a small collection of documents of interest to the Méliès scholar.

Note on translations and abbreviations

Unless otherwise stated, all translations of French quotations are my own, with the exception of film titles, for which I give standard translated versions taken from the British and American Star-Film catalogues.

The conventional abbreviations used in film studies, such as LS (long shot), EC (extreme closeup), and POV (point-of-view shot), are not usually applicable to Méliès. It is tempting, when discussing his films, to use an alternative set of abbreviations: POS (puff of smoke), WD (woman disappears), ME (mayhem ensues), and TSBCB (train swallowed by celestial body). I will refrain, however.

Introduction

Narrative attractions

On 28 December 1895, a barker stood outside the Grand-Café at number 14, boulevard des Capucines shouting at passers-by: 'Entrez, entrez, mesdames et messieurs. Venez voir le cinématographe des frères Lumière de Lyon ... Un franc seulement et vous verrez des personnages grandeur nature s'agiter et vivre sous vos yeux ...'[1] (Malthête-Méliès 1973: 156). Inside, in the basement area known as the Salon Indien, some thirty-five curious spectators, including the director of the popular Grévin wax museum and the head of the Folies-Bergère, took their seats expectantly, waiting to be impressed. Sitting among the specially invited guests was 34-year-old Georges Méliès, magician and director of the Théâtre Robert-Houdin (directly above which Antoine Lumière, father of brothers Auguste and Louis, had a photographic studio). The lights dimmed, and frozen images appeared on the screen. A few moments passed, and the figures remained immobile; members of the audience began to grow restless, and Méliès complained to the person sitting next to him that he didn't see what all the fuss was about. Then, suddenly, the images sprang to life. As Méliès later described that moment, 'No sooner had I stopped speaking when a horse pulling a cart started to walk towards us, followed by

1 'Come on in, ladies and gentlemen. Come see the cinematograph of the Lumière Brothers of Lyon ... For only one franc, you'll see lifesize figures move and come to life before your very eyes ...'

other vehicles, then passers-by – in short, all the hustle and bustle of a street. We sat there with our mouths open, without speaking, filled with amazement' (Toulet 1995: 15).

The effect produced by the first public exhibition of this new invention cannot be overstated. In the early days of cinema, watching a film was not the kind of experience it is today, perceived without thinking as a normal part of daily life; it was an experience unlike any other that had been known before. In 1896, Maxime Gorki described the sense of fear and amazement experienced by many at the earliest film showings: 'Tout à coup, on entend cliqueter quelque chose; tout disparaît, et un train occupe l'écran. Il fonce droit sur nous – attention! On dirait qu'il veut se précipiter dans l'obscurité où nous sommes, faire de nous un infâme amas de chairs déchirées d'os en miettes, et réduire en poussière cette salle et tout ce bâtiment ...' (Prieur 1993: 31).[2] What appeared on the screen seemed real, and this very realism seemed magical – but it was not long before film's seemingly magical effects, such as dissolves, splicing, and multiple exposure, became the basic vocabulary of realist film. Film history is in fact the story of this shift, this process of turning magic into reality; and Méliès is the magician who first performed this feat.

Méliès's place in film history, however, is problematic. Although he is universally acknowledged to be an early film pioneer, his work has often been dismissed as simplistic, both narratively and technically. For a long time, Méliès's work was cited as the foremost example of what Noël Burch termed the 'primitive mode of representation'; films made before around 1906 were characterized, according to Burch, by four traits: the 'autarky and *unicity* of each frame', or framing that is self-contained and unchanged throughout the scene; 'the *noncentered* quality of the image', or the use of the edges of the frame as well as the centre; 'consistent medium long-shot camera distance'; and the '*nonclosure*'

2 'Suddenly, we heard a clicking sound; everything disappeared and a train filled the screen. It was heading right toward us – watch out! You would have thought it wanted to rush out into the dark room in which we were sitting, to turn us into a grotesque pile of torn flesh and shattered bones, reducing to dust the room and the entire building ...'

of the narrative, in other words its reliance on extrafilmic information (such as intertitles, a live commentator, or the audience's familiarity with the film's subject-matter) (Burch 1986: 486–88; original emphasis). In recent years, however, film historians have uncovered mounting evidence of the modernity of very early cinema, illustrated in the use of techniques normally associated with later cinema, such as deep staging and continuity editing. Noël Burch's designation of films made before 1906 as 'primitive' has been superseded by the term 'cinema of attractions', developed by Tom Gunning and André Gaudreault in recognition of the dismissive connotations of the word 'primitive'.[3] Theories of the cinema of attractions ascribe roughly the same characteristics to early film, although they place special emphasis on its presentational or spectacular qualities. As Tom Gunning puts it, '[t]his cinema differs from later narrative cinema through its fascination in the thrill of display rather than its construction of a story' (Elsaesser 1990: 100). Yet even the theorists of the cinema of attractions oversimplify early film, deeming it to be largely devoid of narrative content, rather more 'show' than 'tell'.

The distinction of 'primitive' par excellence has always been reserved for Méliès, whose *féeries* or fantasy films have helped categorize him as an imaginative but unsophisticated pioneer of early cinema. Méliès is the filmmaker whose position in film history would be the most affected by a reassessment of early film. David Bordwell acknowledges that film editing was 'pioneered by Méliès', but qualifies this statement by adding that 'however, these techniques are not necessarily steps toward the perfection of film narrative; storytelling was only one purpose of Méliès' *féeries*, and his editing often served to heighten legerdemain and theatrical spectacle' (Bordwell 1997: 33 and 128). Although Bordwell's assessment of Méliès's place in film history is one of the best informed, the narrative content that he concedes on the one hand is dismissed on the other as it is relegated to the domain

3 For Burch's proposal of the term 'primitive cinema', see 'A Primitive Mode of Representation?' in Elsaesser 1990: 220. For a discussion of the term 'cinema of attractions', see Gunning, 'The Cinema of Attractions: Early Film, Its Spectator and the Avant-Garde', also in Elsaesser 1990.

of theatrical spectacle. Richard Abel makes a similar compromise in his magisterial study of early French film, *The Ciné Goes to Town*. He first discusses Méliès's work under the heading 'cinema of attractions'; but then, in the following chapter titled 'The Transition to a Narrative Cinema', he inserts another section on Méliès labelled 'The Cinema of Attractions (continued)' (Abel 1998: 156 ff.). The awkwardness of this insertion points to the tension between the narrative content in Méliès's films and the widespread tendency among film scholars to classify them as cinema of attractions.

Other recent reappraisals of early cinema make a similar gesture toward recognizing the narrative content of Méliès's films only ultimately to dismiss it. In a 1995 essay, Tom Gunning concedes that it is probably not possible to assign early films exclusively either to the realm of attractions or to that of narration, but then adds that narrative content in the trick films 'semble néanmoins principalement fonctionner de la même manière que le décor Louis XV lui-même, c'est-à-dire comme une sorte de cadre pour le véritable intérêt du film: le processus d'apparition, de disparition, de transformation et de réapparition'.[4] Gunning insists on attributing authorial intention ('the film's true subject') to Méliès in a way that would not be acceptable today in the context of later films (or in the context of literary texts of any period). Charles Musser offers a corrective to Gunning's dichotomy between attractions and narration, contending that, 'En fait, les attractions et la narration sont efficacement combinées puisque les coups de théâtre que Méliès adorait font également partie de la narration'.[5] But for all of his effective championing of Méliès's modernity, Musser quickly drops Méliès in order to turn his

4 'nevertheless seems to function principally like the Louis XV decor, that is, like a kind of frame for the film's true subject: the process of appearance, disappearance, transformation and reappearance'. (Tom Gunning, 'Attractions, truquages et photogénie: l'explosion du présent dans les films à truc français produits entre 1896 et 1907' in Gili, Lagny *et al.* 1995: 183 and 185.)

5 'In fact, attractions and narrative are efficiently combined because the theatrical turns that Méliès favoured are also an integral part of the narration'. (Charles Musser, 'Pour une nouvelle approche du cinéma des premiers temps: le cinéma d'attractions et la narrativité' in Gili, Lagny *et al.* 1995: 155.)

attention to highlighting the narrative dimension in the films of Edwin Porter, which, he argues, has previously been overshadowed by an excessive emphasis placed on Griffith (Gili, Lagny, *et al.* 1995: 169–70). The case Musser makes for Porter is equally applicable to Méliès, but he does not go so far as to show this. That Musser has different priorities is by no means grounds for reproach; but now that all of the seeds have been planted for establishing the narrative force of Méliès's films, it seems that the time has come to take the project one step further. Marshall Deutelbaum has made a compelling case for elements of narrative structure in many of the Lumière films previously considered to be totally devoid of narrative content (Deutelbaum 1979); one of the aims of this study is to make a similar case for the work of Méliès.

There is no question that Méliès's films contain elements of spectacle, or 'attractions'. But the presence of spectacle in no way detracts from the films' narrative content – their internal hetero-geneity only links them more closely to the vast majority of films that came after them. Rather than what Gunning calls the 'heterogeneous relation that film before 1906 (or so) bears to the films that follow' (Elsaesser 1990: 56), I wish to posit a certain homogeneity among films made prior to and after 1906 by locating a certain heterogeneity *within* individual films made by Méliès. As feminist and other film theorists have demonstrated, storytelling is only ever a single component of any film; the notion of 'visual pleasure' developed by Laura Mulvey (Mulvey 1975) surely applies to any spectacular element of a film, from lush scenery to magic tricks designed to amaze and delight. Although Méliès certainly exploited visual pleasure in the specific sense in which Mulvey intended it, in his repeated images of scantily-clad young women, he also promoted visual pleasure in a broader sense, but *within a narrative context*. Rather than a progression from recording (Lumière) to spectacle (Méliès) to narrative (nearly everyone who followed, with the exception of certain avant-garde filmmakers), film history is made up of different combinations of all three elements. Méliès's films, like most films, both show *and* tell (or 'monstrate' and narrate, as André Gaudreault puts it (Elsaesser 1990: 276)), creating meaning as they entertain.

This book, therefore, aims to dispel a number of myths about Méliès's contribution to film history. These myths, which sometimes overlap and sometimes contradict one another – as myths do – are the following:

Myth 1   Méliès made primarily fairytales and fantasies characterized by their childlike naiveté.

Myth 2   Méliès's style is exclusively theatrical, with little or nothing in the way of specifically cinematic features or effects.

Myth 3   Méliès's work is largely devoid of narrative structure and symbolic coherence, and is therefore qualitatively different from that of most filmmakers who followed him. His films may not, therefore, be analyzed using the tools of modern film theory.

To some extent, these myths were fostered by Méliès himself. His lifelong struggle for artistic independence and creative control over his work extended to the legend that grew up around him – but this would eventually turn against him. Like the running story lines that Méliès brought to disparate tricks in his magic acts, the seminal moments that punctuate his life can be strung together to form a cohesive narrative, bringing a sense of purpose and meaning to what might otherwise appear as little more than a series of spectacular feats. This narrative may be called Méliès's Life Story.

Life Story

Marie-Georges-Jean Méliès (known as Georges) was born in Paris on 8 December 1861, the youngest by many years of three children. His mother, Johannah Catherine Schuering (known as Catherine), was a native of Holland, and his father, Jean-Louis-Stanislas Méliès (known as Louis), had become a prosperous footwear manufacturer. Catherine Méliès was 42 years old when her youngest son was born, and the boot business that she and her husband had worked hard to build was flourishing, allowing her the leisure to lavish the better part of her time and attention on her youngest son. She was determined that Georges should obtain his *baccalauréat*, unlike his brothers, whom the family had not had the means to send away to preparatory schools. At the age of seven, Georges was sent to board at the Lycée du Prince Impérial in Vanves. He already displayed a talent for drawing and puppetry, skills that would later serve him well in his film-making career. With the onslaught of the Franco-Prussian War in 1870, Méliès was evacuated to the Lycée Louis-le-Grand, where he obtained his *baccalauréat* in 1880. After a year of military service (November 1881–November 1882, a three-year obligation cut short by a 1,500–franc 'donation' to the armed services),[6] Méliès hoped fervently to train at the École des Beaux-Arts to become a painter, but his father insisted that he join the family business instead. Father and son were both adamant, so the only solution was a compromise: Georges would not attend the École des Beaux-Arts, but he would be allowed to take private art lessons – provided, according to his granddaughter Madeleine Malthête-Méliès (1973: 49 ff.), by the painter Gustave Moreau[7] – as long as he also devoted several hours a day to overseeing the mechanical functioning of the boot factory. Although he could not have foreseen it at the time, this compromise, which provided him with equal parts artistic and technical training, would provide him with many of the tools he would need in his future career as a filmmaker. But Méliès, who was mechanically adept and handled his factory responsibilities capably, longed to be able to devote himself entirely to creative pursuits.

In 1884 he went to London, for the purposes of learning English and establishing contacts for the London branch of the shoe business that the family would open soon afterwards. By all accounts, the year he spent in London was to alter the course of Méliès's life.

While working first in a shoe store and then in a clothing boutique, Méliès sought diversion in London's theatrical productions. His limited command of English, especially at the beginning of his stay, steered him toward the kinds of productions that relied largely on visual spectacle: pantomime and magic acts. The

6 Paul Hammond (1974: 14) contends that Méliès spent over three years in the military, but all other sources give one year.

7 Hammond (1974: 15) questions this assertion.

English 'pantos' that Méliès would have seen in London that season included *Red Riding Hood*, *The Golden Ring*, and *Cinderella* – the latter containing a scene in which 'the fairy Electra ... flew down bearing the glass slippers' (Robinson 1993: 6), a sight that no doubt contributed to Méliès's cinematic interest in flying women. The enchanted worlds depicted in these spectacles, and the lavish decors and special effects featured in them, appealed to Méliès's sense of whimsy. The fantastical creatures that appeared in these spectacles were unfettered by the laws of physics that constrained real human beings; here, if it could be imagined, it could be done.

While in London, Méliès became a devotee of Maskelyne and Cooke's Egyptian Hall, a theatre specializing in conjuring and magic acts. Here he was befriended by John Nevil Maskelyne, one of the most renowned British illusionists of the day, who wove magic tricks into a narrative structure, thereby alternately amusing and amazing his audiences. Méliès soon attempted to replicate the techniques of Maskelyne and of another great magician, David Devant, who was known for making a life-sized portrait of a woman appear to come to life. (This illusion would become the basis of Méliès's 1903 film *Le Portrait spirite/The Spiritualist Photographer*.) Similarly, Joseph Buatier de Kolta's famous illusion, 'The Vanishing Lady', in which a seated woman disappeared from beneath a cloth that had been draped over her, would later be recreated by Méliès, first on stage, and then in the 1896 film *L'Escamotage d'une dame chez Robert-Houdin/The Vanishing Lady*.)

Upon his return to Paris in 1885, Méliès pursued his new-found interest in magic, practising feverishly until he was able to perform illusions in front of friends and family and then, after only a couple of years, at the Musée Grévin and the Galerie Vivienne. His 1885 marriage to Eugénie Genin, the daughter of a wealthy family friend, provided him with a large dowry, enabling Méliès to develop his conjuring talents without the burden, initially, of needing to earn a living. In 1888, Louis Méliès retired from the family business, dividing it among his three sons. Georges sold his share to his brothers for a sum that, combined with some of his wife's money, enabled him to purchase the

Théâtre Robert-Houdin – named after the celebrated French magician, Jean-Eugène Robert-Houdin, who had died in 1871 – on the Boulevard des Italiens.

Robert-Houdin was an inspiration to generations of magicians, from Méliès to the American illusionist who adopted the stage name Harry Houdini. His theatre was equipped with a whole range of trap doors, pulleys, mechanical devices and elaborate constructions used for performing illusions, all of which were included with the sale of the premises. So, in 1888, the young would-be magician (and wouldn't-be shoemaker) found himself in charge of a small but illustrious theatre, which he refurbished and reopened in autumn of that year. Méliès was to manage, design sets, invent tricks for, and perform in the Théâtre Robert-Houdin off and on until 1915, when financial difficulties eventually forced him to sell it to a cinema operator.

Shortly after he purchased the Robert-Houdin, political events compelled Méliès to divert his attention briefly to weightier matters. This was the height of Boulangism, which offended Méliès's republican sympathies: in 1889, General Boulanger, who enjoyed enormous populist support, came very close to over-throwing the Third Republic and reinstating a form of monarchy. Méliès's devotion to the art of illusion did not prevent him from showing an interest in the very real world of politics; so it was that from August 1889 to February 1890, he drew satirical cartoons under the anagrammatic pseudonym of Geo Smile for the anti-Boulangist journal *La Griffe*, published by his cousin Adolphe. This act of committed artistry prefigured the political partisanship he was to demonstrate in his pro-Dreyfus film series, *L'Affaire Dreyfus/The Dreyfus Affair*, in 1899.

Otherwise, however, the period from 1888 to 1895 was devoted almost entirely to running his theatre. The programme at the Robert-Houdin included magic tricks, *féeries* or fantasy panto-mime spectacles, and displays of the automats that Méliès had inherited when he purchased the Robert-Houdin – mechanized robots who entertained spectators between acts. Many of the illusions performed by Méliès were inspired by the work of Robert-Houdin himself as well as other magicians, but Méliès quickly began designing original illusions, many of them featuring Jehanne d'Alcy, who would go on to star in his films (and to become his second wife in 1925). His first creation, *La Stroubaika persane*, involved tying a collaborator to a plank, covering him and suspending him in mid-air. After emitting mysterious musical sounds, the collaborator would then appear, miraculously, among the audience, while the clamps and bonds on the plank remained unbroken (Malthête-Méliès 1973: 103). Other illusions included *L'Enchanteur Alcofribas* (which had little in common with the 1903 film of the same name), in which the eponymous character chased after his own head as it was being carried off by a skeleton, and *Le Décapité récalcitrant*, which featured an overly loquacious professor whose head is cut off and placed in a box, from where it continues its chatty monologue. In 1891, Méliès created and presided over the Académie de Prestidigitation; between 1888 and 1907, both before and during his film career, he created some thirty illusions, some of whose mechanical features he marketed with a friend, the theatrical supplier Voisin. Although his talents and interests took him through many phases of a long and varied career, Méliès would always remain a magician of one kind or another.

Moving pictures

Méliès's move into film did not come entirely out of the blue. Years before he witnessed the first public film screening at the Grand Café, he was already experimenting with slide projections. The programme at the Robert-Houdin included magic-lantern shows, which featured chromatropes (two painted glass slides turned in opposite directions to produce kaleidoscope effects) and mechanized slides that could be made to move horizontally or dissolve into one another, prefiguring the lap dissolve in the cinema. In 1892, Méliès saw the 'pantomimes lumineuses' at the Musée Grévin, the world's first animated drawings projected onto a screen by Emile Reynaud's Théâtre Optique. The Théâtre Optique was an advanced version of the praxinoscope, a mirrored cylinder within a larger, revolving band of images projected onto a screen, which Reynaud had patented in 1877 (*Emile Reynaud Peintre de films* 1945: 8). Reynaud's invention came very close to cinema, but it used animated illustrations rather than photographs.

Meanwhile, other experiments in moving pictures were being carried out both in France and abroad. These experiments were building on the work of predecessors such as the British photographer Eadweard James Muybridge, whose sequential snapshots allowed him to reconstruct the movement of animals and humans, and whose work was in turn based largely on that of Etienne-Jules Marey, a French physiologist who began recording images on a long strip of photographic paper instead of on individual plates. In 1891, the American inventor Thomas Edison, working with the Englishman William Kennedy Laurie Dickson, developed the kinetoscope, a device modelled largely on Marey's earlier machine, with a peephole through which an individual could view moving photographs. Edison made one-minute films for his kinetoscope with the camera he had developed, to which he gave the complementary name of kinetograph. The individual viewing stations may have prefigured the atomized spectatorship later created by television, but because Edison's films could not be projected onto a screen they did not yet constitute the cinematic experience as we now know it.

The work of two brothers from Lyons named Louis and Auguste Lumière, however, certainly did qualify as cinema. In order to perfect what they would call the *cinématographe*, Louis had developed a feed mechanism that regulated the intermittent advancement of film so that an individual frame paused at the exact moment the shutter opened, thus permitting the projection of the image onto a screen. (Ironically, it was not until they discovered how to stop motion for a split second that the inventors were able to convey the impression of movement.) The Lumières' creation was a multipurpose machine that filmed, printed, and projected moving images at sixteen frames per second. Although the Lumières were not strictly the first people to show film to the public (they had been beaten to it by Max Skladanowsky, who had exhibited his Bioskop in Berlin in early November of the same year), they were the first to gain worldwide attention for this achievement. Alan Williams has argued that, in addition to their undisputed technical acumen, what really set the Lumières apart from others working on similar projects at the time was their capacity as 'talented entrepreneurs' (Fell 1983: 153). In any case, there is no doubt that suddenly, at the end of 1895, the number of people who could watch the same moving images was limited only by the space available in the screening room: so the social phenomenon of cinema was born. It was this phenomenon, with its capacity to thrill and amaze (not to mention extract money from) audiences, that Méliès witnessed in the Salon des Indiens on 28 December 1895. As he sat spellbound in that darkened room, the master illusionist realized that the power of film was no illusion: 'Nous étions tous absolument stupéfaits. Immédiatement j'ai dit "Voilà mon affaire ... un truc extraordinaire!"' (Malthête-Méliès 1973: 157).[8] Méliès decided that he had to acquire that power for himself.

Despite making repeated offers to Antoine Lumière, (going up to the considerable sum of 10,000 francs), Méliès's efforts to purchase a *cinématographe* did not meet with success. The father of the machine's inventors (and thus the grandfather of cinema) felt that interest in the new medium would be short-lived, and that it would be best for the family to exploit it exclusively until its popularity waned. Although history was to prove Lumière wrong – that is, at least as far as the endurance of the invention's appeal was concerned – Méliès was nonetheless left, quite literally, to his own devices.

He travelled to London, where he managed to purchase a projector from the inventor Robert William Paul for 1,000 francs. This machine, called the Animatograph, was actually an 'unauthorized kinetoscope' (Williams 1992: 21), which Edison could not prevent from being manufactured and distributed in Europe because his own work had been based heavily on Marey's ideas. In April 1896, Méliès began projecting short films, purchased from Paul and from the Edison Company, at the Théâtre

---

8 'We were all positively stupefied. I immediately said, "That's the thing for me ... an extraordinary trick!"'

Robert-Houdin. The Animatograph was much clumsier than the Lumières' machine, and Méliès, borrowing also from the Isola Brothers' Isolatograph, worked on improving it with two associates, Lucien Reulos and Lucien Korsten. The three were soon able to patent the 'Méliès-Reulos Kinetograph', a combined camera-projector made from mechanical parts found in his theatre's storeroom. In May or June of that year (accounts differ), Méliès made his first film in his family's garden in Montreuil, a suburb of Paris. *Une Partie de cartes/Playing Cards*, seventeen metres and less than a minute long, was an imitation of the Lumière brothers' *Partie d'Écarté*, starring Méliès, his brother Gaston, and a couple of friends. Méliès continued to make Lumière-inspired, slice-of-life films, sometimes setting up little naturalistic scenes, at other times going out and shooting footage of his surroundings or filming newsworthy events such as the Russian tsar's visit to Paris or the 1900 world's fair. To these, however, he soon added staged films – what were then called *scènes composées*, or artifically arranged scenes – with more elaborate sets and costumes.

In addition to showing his 'vues de la maison' at the Théâtre Robert-Houdin, Méliès also sold them to the operators of makeshift cinemas that were springing up in fairgrounds, or *fêtes foraines*, all over France. For many years, films were slotted into varied programmes of entertainment that included attractions as diverse as musical and dance numbers, acrobats, and demon-strations of technological marvels such as x-ray machines. Cinema's lack of exclusive billing among so many atractions was mirrored to some extent in the absence of credits at either the beginning or the end of films. Similarly, the first film stars, like the first films, were anonymous. As Méliès himself wrote in idiosyncratic English after his film career had ended, 'there were not yet "Stars" amongst the artists, their name was never known nor written on bills or advertisements. The film was named – Starfilm – and the name Méliès, itself, did not appear on the screen, though I performed the principal characters' (Méliès (?), 'Copie à une réponse ...'). Thus, early film's primary appeal lay not in the star quality of its actors or the satisfaction derived from a well-crafted script (in fact, most of Méliès's early films did not even use scripts); instead, film often served as a demonstration of the new medium itself. Cinema was still new to many people in rural settings for years after its invention, and it was often considered a thrill merely to see such a marvellous thing for oneself.

But to those who had already witnessed the flickering of shadowy images across a screen, the novelty soon wore off, and cinema became just another form of entertainment vying for the public's attention. It was apparent that film would have to do more than just point to its own existence if it was to hold people's interest. Méliès soon began developing the medium's performative and narrative potential, producing works that were more in keeping with the other kinds of spectacles he presented at his theatre. He would later write, at the end of his film career, of this idea 'de faire servir le cinéma, non à la reproduction servile de la nature, mais à l'expression spectaculaire des conceptions artistiques et imaginatives de tous genres' (Méliès 1912: 1–2).[9] In order to achieve this 'expression spectaculaire', he needed a theatre specially equipped to accommodate filming: at the end of 1896, he began building, and in the spring of 1897, he opened, the world's first permanent film studio on the family's grounds at Montreuil, outside of Paris. From then on, nearly all of his films would be shot indoors in this studio, which resembled a large greenhouse. Before its subsequent expansions, the studio measured seventeen metres long, six metres wide, and six metres high at its tallest point – virtually the same dimensions as the Théâtre Robert-Houdin. Méliès eventually equipped his studio, as well, like the Robert-Houdin, installing trap doors, trick panels and ramps, which would enable him to produce the *féeries* or fantasies for which he came to be known. The walls and ceiling of the studio were made of glass to allow maximum light to enter, and the wall behind the stage was equipped with shutters to prevent light from entering when it was not wanted. (Like Edison, Méliès initially had to rely on natural light.) In 1905, he was to build a second studio, which he called Studio B, next to the first.

9 'of using cinema, not for the servile reproduction of nature, but for the spectacular expression of artistic and creative ideas of all kinds'.

In 1897, Méliès started up his own production company, Star-Film. Over the next fifteen years, he would make some 520 films (of which only about 170 are known to have survived), in genres as diverse as documentary, staged re-enactments of current events, erotic or 'stag' films, *féeries*, 'trick' films and science fiction. Méliès also began making filmed advertisements, the first in Europe, in 1898, which he projected onto the sides of buildings with the help of his daughter Georgette who, as a child, worked as a projectionist for her father. Most of these films used trick photography and had a whimsical, even comical, tone. The advertisement for Delion hats showed rabbits going through a machine and emerging as hats before turning back into rabbits, suggesting that, for Méliès the magician, hats were inevitably associated with rabbits, but also sending up the mechanized magic that is cinema. In a film for Dewar's whisky, painted portraits come to life, emerge from their frames and have a drink, anticipating Méliès's 1906 film *Les Affiches en goguette/The Hilarious Posters*. And to promote a treatment for baldness, Méliès rubs lotion on his head, and, werewolf-like, both his head and his hands are suddenly covered with tufts of hair (Hammond 1974: 35–6). In another publicity film, diners in a restaurant become involved in a food fight, splattering Bornibus mustard on each other, which a dog licks up hungrily (Méliès actually used chocolate-flavoured cream). In their use of humour, the advertisements were perfectly in keeping with Méliès's fiction films, the majority of which, regardless of their formal genre, were characterized by their irreverent playfulness.

The business side of Méliès's career, however, was no laughing matter. For eight or nine years he prospered, selling his films at home and abroad. But eventually his competitors, both French and American, caught up with him. The more famous his films became, the more his competitors pirated them, especially in the United States. Bootleg copies of his most successful film, the 1902 *Voyage dans la lune/A Trip to the Moon*, were manufactured and sold all over the world with the Star-Film logo removed, and Méliès saw only a fraction of the film's profits. Although flattered by this tribute to the film's popularity, Méliès nonetheless realized that he would have to safeguard his financial interests. In 1903, he sent his brother Gaston to New York to open a branch office responsible for registering his films for US copyright, and for selling prints directly to the American market. Méliès then began producing two nearly identical negative prints of each film by setting up two cameras side by side (one of which was often operated by his daughter Georgette) and filming the same scene simultaneously. One of the negatives remained in France and the other was sent to the United States, where Gaston made copies for American distribution, simultaneously depositing a paper print for copyright in the Library of Congress.[10]

Meanwhile, Méliès also faced stiff domestic competition from Pathé, who had started out as a fairground exhibitor but who eventually began renting out his films instead of selling them. Until then fairground exhibitors had purchased films, which they showed repeatedly until they wore out, because they were sure of finding new audiences as they travelled around France. The new rental arrangement was institutionalized in 1909 at the Congrès International des Fabricants de Films over which Méliès presided, a position that was more a tribute to his film-making skills than to his business acumen, and which would prove cruelly ironic, considering the harm that the decision reached at the meeting would do to his production company. The new arrangement benefited producers who could make films quickly and cheaply, like Pathé, whose production far exceeded that of Méliès (eighteen titles monthly in 1905/6 compared to two titles per month from Méliès) (Malthête 1996: 147). Méliès's artisanal style and financial independence gave him complete artistic control over his films, allowing him to pay meticulous attention to detail, but the industry was coming to require ever-expanding volume rather than high production values. Méliès had to find new formats, and new audiences, for his films. In 1905 and 1906, he created short films to accompany multi-media theatrical productions at the Théâtre du Châtelet (the 'celestial carriage' scene from *Les Quat'cents farces du diable/The Merry Frolics of Satan*) and the Folies-Bergère (*Le*

10 See Malthête 1989: 9–11.

Raid Paris-Monte Carlo en deux heures/An Adventurous Automobile Trip). These films were intercalated between scenes performed live. During and after Méliès's career, as films became more fragmented – cut up and 'sutured' together in the editing room – so did the production process, which was broken up into increasingly specialized roles. Méliès was an *auteur* in the true sense – in that he was personally involved in every aspect of production, from script-writing, design and construction of the elaborate sets, and lighting, to directing, acting, development of film stock, editing, and writing promotional materials. Such absolute independence would never again be possible – not even when filmmakers such as Truffaut and Godard were hailed as the 'authors' of films that employed sizeable production teams, although they personally performed only a few of the functions that Méliès did.

Meanwhile, Thomas Edison had begun his campaign to monopolize the American market by waging legal battles against anyone who attempted to produce or sell films there, arguing that, as the first holder of an American patent for film-making equipment, he was entitled to control all of the country's film production. In early 1908, the Motion Picture Patents Company (MPPC) was formed. This was a cartel composed of the major patent holders which controlled every aspect of film production. In 1915, the MPPC was ruled to be an illegal trust by a US Federal district court but, until then, it managed to thwart the growth of independent producers (including Méliès). Nonetheless, in the hope of competing in the American market, Star-Film, represented by Gaston Méliès, reluctantly joined the MPPC, as did Pathé. In order to remain in the cartel, Méliès was required to supply the American market, which had witnessed an explosion of nickelodeon theatres, with 1,000 feet (some 300 metres) of film per week. Méliès worked at a frantic pace in 1908, more than tripling his average annual production. This was especially hard on him, because his involvement in nearly every aspect of production meant that he worked more slowly than his competitors. Consequently, the prices of his films were considerably higher than those of his rivals – for example, his films were 30–50 per cent more expensive than those sold by Pathé before he began renting.[11] The mass production and rapid turnover of films required by an increasingly insatiable market did not suit Méliès's artisanal approach.

To take some of the burden of the increased production requirements off his brother, Gaston Méliès began making films on behalf of the American branch of Star-Film. Based first in Fort Lee, New Jersey, across the bridge from Manhattan and not far from Edison's studios in West Orange, the firm moved its base of operations to San Antonio, Texas in 1910, where Gaston specialised in Westerns filmed in the surrounding landscape, and changed the name of the company's American branch to American Wildwest. However, the new outfit was as restless and as full of wanderlust as the cowboys it filmed, because the next year it packed up and moved even farther west, to an arid, undeveloped region of southern California. At first, the new company prospered, making over 130 films between 1910 and 1912. In the summer of 1912, Gaston embarked on a world tour in order to film 'exotic' locales in the South Pacific, but inadequate facilities and a series of mishaps led to financial ruin. He was forced to liquidate the company in 1913; in 1915, he died of food poisoning in Corsica.

By 1911, in order to continue making films, Georges Méliès had had to sacrifice his financial and creative independence by agreeing to hand over his finished work to Charles Pathé, who provided him with financing. The films were subjected to heavy editing by Pathé's director, Ferdinand Zecca. This horrified and outraged Méliès, who had never had to yield creative control of his work to anyone. Moreover, audiences were losing interest in his films, which had not adapted to reflect changing tastes; what critics consider to be one of his finest films, the 1912 *A la conquête du Pôle/The Conquest of the Pole*, was virtually ignored at the time of its release. Méliès was finally forced to stop production, and faced losing his Montreuil studio to creditors, an eventuality that would be delayed until 1923 as a result of the First World War.

11 See Jacques Malthête, 'Historiographie méliésienne' (Malthête and Marie 1997: 32).

During the war years, Méliès wrote and performed in variety shows with his daughter Georgette, his son André and their spouses. In 1917, his business office in the passage de l'Opéra was requisitioned by the army, which seized approximately 400 films and melted them down in order to produce a chemical used in the production of boot heels – as has often been noted, this was a sad irony for the son of a shoe merchant.

The demise of Star-Film coincided with the decline of the French film industry, which would never regain the power and influence it had exercised before the First World War, when it dominated world markets.[12] The film historian Maurice Noverre summed up Méliès's role in the history of the *septième art* in a personal letter to Méliès dated 29 July 1929: 'L. Lumière a *fait l'outil* [amended at bottom of page: '*mis au point* plutôt']; avec cet outil, vous avez créé un art continué par les Américains'.[13] In forming one of the world's first film production companies, Méliès was instrumental in commodifying the art of (film) magic – yet it was this very commodification that led to his financial ruin. He refused to conform to the exigencies of the industry he had helped create.

Méliès scraped together a living in the years immediately following the war by doing odd jobs and performing in touring variety shows. In 1925, he remarried (his first wife Eugenie had died in 1913): his new bride, Jehanne d'Alcy (the stage name of Fanny Manieux, born Charlotte-Stéphane Faes), was herself a widow, a longtime mistress of Méliès and star of many of his films and even earlier magic acts. D'Alcy had recently purchased a toy and sweets concession in the Gare Montparnasse, which she and Méliès ran until 1932, working and living in obscurity. Then, in 1929, several of Méliès's films were discovered in a house belonging to a wealthy furniture store owner who had, years earlier, commissioned Méliès to make films that could be shown

---

12 For a history of the French film industry up to this point, see Abel 1998: 10–58.

13 'L. Lumière created the tool [amended to read: 'or perfected it, rather']; and with this tool, you have created an artform continued by the Americans' (Fonds Méliès, Collection Cinémathèque Française, BiFi, MÉLIÈS 4; original emphasis).

to children while their mothers shopped. These films were restored and shown on 16 December of that year in the Salle Pleyel, at a glittery gala in honour of Méliès. The fact that the films shown at this high-profile event were predominantly fairy tales made expressly for children helped foster the widely-held but inaccurate assumption that Méliès only made childlike fantasies. In 1931, he was awarded the Cross of the Legion of Honour, which was pinned on his chest by none other than Louis Lumière. In 1932, Méliès was given the use of an apartment in Orly, into which he moved with D'Alcy and his granddaughter (whose mother, Méliès's daughter Georgette, had died after a long illness), but he still struggled to make ends meet.

Although his importance in the history of cinema had been acknowledged by the film industry, his life continued in much the same way as it had since the war, albeit punctuated by visits from film historians and other admirers, including several surrealists, who admired Méliès's work for its irreverence and for its challenge to the conventions of realism. They were doubtless drawn to the apparent spontaneity and incongruity of Méliès's trick substitution effects, which prefigured the surrealist fondness for throwing together ostensibly unrelated objects into a context completely different from that in which they were normally found. This artistic continuity no doubt accounts for the fact that the surrealists embraced Méliès in the 1920s, when he was still out of favour with everyone else. At the time of his death, of cancer, on 21 January 1938, he was involved in discussions with Marcel Carné for a film about a phantom of the métro, and there were plans to collaborate with the dadaist artist Hans Richter on a new version of *Munchausen*.

One reason for Méliès's decline in popularity is perhaps that his ebullient antics were more suited to the *belle époque* than to the dark cynicism that enveloped France on the eve of the Great War. Méliès's films were often ironic and comical, but rarely cynical. After the war, avant-garde filmmakers would pay tribute to Méliès in their own productions, which alluded to the film pioneer's work as nostalgically (and parodically) as Méliès himself had invoked the marvellous innocence of an earlier age. For example, René

Clair's 1926 *Voyage imaginaire* includes a scene set in a home for ageing fairies, in which sooty-faced elderly women dressed in rags wear little star tiaras in their hair, and Blue Beard, Cinderella, Prince Charming and Puss-in-Boots appear as old-age pensioners. An intertitle reads: 'No one believes in fairies anymore. So my sisters have been shut away in this retreat'.[14]

Although a product of his era – Méliès was heavily influenced by his origins in the magic theatre – his films were innovative and responsible for anticipating and influencing every major current of film-making in the twentieth century. Méliès has been at the centre of important debates about the development of cinematic form and style, and his work has provoked both adoration and disdain. Some dismiss him as naive, but the primary aim of this book is to give an idea of the complexity – and modernity – of his work. Accordingly, the first chapter outlines the technical function of the major special effects, or *trucs*, used by Méliès. The chapter then progresses to a structural analysis of the narrative components of Méliès's films, by adapting Christian Metz's model known as *la grande syntagmatique* to a spatial model of mise en scène. The aim of this exercise is two-fold: first, it reveals the narrative complexity of Méliès's films; and, in so doing, it demonstrates that early cinema need not be excluded from analysis using the tools of modern film theory. In using a structuralist model for demonstration purposes, I have chosen a seminal but somewhat dated approach, but the implication is that other, more recent analytical tools (post- or post-post-structuralist) may be similarly illuminating.

Chapter 2, 'Fantastic realism', considers the ways in which Méliès's films blur the boundary between realism and illusion, by examining first a selection of trick films, followed by several *actualités reconstituées* or early docu-dramas, culminating in an extended discussion of Méliès's most influential actualité, *L'Affaire Dreyfus/The Dreyfus Affair* (1899), which heralded film's accession to the historical role once performed exclusively by writing.

14 This English translation appears on the NFA's copy of the film.

Chapter 3, 'The amazing flying woman', takes up Méliès's treatment of gender roles, focusing specifically on the fairies and other airborne women who people his films, which reflected attitudes towards women that were prevalent in French culture at the turn of the century.

Chapter 4 examines several of Méliès's voyage films, which, although whimsical, suggested that the developing technologies of motion that were bringing people closer together did not put an end to the social divisions and cultural prejudices that were driving them apart.

Finally, in a brief conclusion, I review the central myths surrounding Méliès's work, in light of the arguments I have made to disprove them. While taking account of the fact that Méliès's films reflected many conventions and preoccupations of the time, this study will focus primarily on Méliès's role as an innovator and storyteller, as the magician who made modern cinema appear before our very eyes.

References

Abel, Richard (1998), *The Ciné Goes to Town*, Berkeley, CA, University of California Press.

Bordwell, D. (1997), *On the History of Film Style*, Cambridge, MA, Harvard University Press.

Burch, Noël (1986), 'Primitivism and the Avant-Gardes: A Dialectical Approach', in Rosen, Philip (ed.), *Narrative, Apparatus, Ideology*, New York, Columbia University Press, 483–506.

Deutelbaum, M. (1979), 'Structural Patterning in the Lumière Films', *Wide Angle* 3:1.

Elsaesser, T. (ed.) (1990), *Early Cinema: Space, Frame, Narrative*, London, British Film Institute.

Emile Reynaud Peintre de films (1945), Paris, Cinémathèque Française.

Fell, J. L. (ed.) (1983), *Film Before Griffith*, Berkeley, CA, University of California Press.

Gili, J. A., Lagny, M. *et al.* (eds.) (1995), *Les Vingt premières années du cinéma français*, Paris, Presses de la Sorbonne Nouvelle.

Hammond, P. (1974), *Marvellous Méliès*, London, Gordon Fraser.

Malthête, Jacques (1989), 'Les Actualités reconstituées de Georges Méliès', *Archives* 21, mars, Institut Jean Vigo-Cinémathèque Toulouse.

—— (1996), *Méliès, images et illusions*, Paris, Exporégie.

Malthête, J. and Marie, M. (eds.) (1997), *Georges Méliès l'illusionniste fin de siècle?* Paris, Presses de la Sorbonne Nouvelle.

Malthête-Méliès, M. (1973), *Méliès l'Enchanteur*, Paris, Hachette.

Méliès, Georges (n.d.), 'Copie à une réponse de Méliès à des questions, relatif au film "Voyage dans la lune", posées à Méliès par Jean A. LeRoy' in BiFi Fonds Méliès GM003 (nonpaginated).

Méliès, Georges (1912), 'Le Merveilleux au cinéma', *L'Echo du cinéma* 24 mai.

Mulvey, L. (1975), 'Visual Pleasure and Narrative Cinema', *Screen* 16:3.

Prieur, J. (1993), *Le Spectateur nocturne*, Paris, Editions de l'Etoile/Cahiers du cinéma.

Robinson, D. (1993), *Georges Méliès: Father of Film Fantasy*, London, British Film Institute.

Toulet, E. (1995) *Cinema is 100 Years Old*, trans. S. Emanuel, London, Thames and Hudson Ltd.

Williams, Alan (1992), *Republic of Images: A History of French Film-making*, Cambridge, MA, Harvard University Press.

Méliès does tricks

In *Le Boulevard du cinéma à l'époque de Georges Méliès*, Jacques Deslandes voiced a common view of Méliès's contribution to cinema: 'Méliès n'est pas un pionnier du cinéma, mais le dernier homme du théâtre de féerie' (71).[1] This assessment of Méliès's work still persists today, and can be traced back at least as far as 1947 when Georges Sadoul, who wrote the earliest serious study of Méliès's work, called Méliès a 'prisonnier ... des charmes du théâtre' (Sadoul 1947: 23).[2] Although the perception of Méliès as essentially a man of the theatre who happened to point a camera at the stage has long held sway, I intend here to provide a more complex assessment of Méliès's film techniques. Méliès may have perpetuated traditions of the past, but he was just as firmly turned toward the future. To be sure, he performed magic in front of the camera, often filming his own disappearing acts; but, more significantly for the history of film, he also performed magic in the editing room, which enabled him to create effects that were both spectacular and narratively motivated.

Any discussion of special effects, however, must first take account of the state of film-making technology in the early days of the medium's existence. One of the most significant factors in early film production was the limitation imposed by the reliance on natural light. The Lumière brothers' early films were shot out

---

1 'Méliès is not a pioneer of the cinema, but rather the last practitioner of the theatrical fantasy play.'
2 'prisoner of the theatre's charms'.

of doors, as were Méliès's first films. The world's first film studio, Edison's 'Black Maria', had been built on a rotating train turntable so that the ramshackle structure could be turned to follow the sun's path through the sky, like an enormous sunflower. Méliès's studios were airy glass-and-iron structures modelled on nineteenth-century photographic studios, which in turn had been modelled on greenhouses (they also resembled the glass-roofed, iron-veined arcades about which Walter Benjamin was to write so eloquently (1978: 147)). Méliès installed large blinds on the ceiling, which he could manipulate from the ground via a pulley system, in order to block out some of the light when it cast distracting shadows, especially in the summer months. Although he experimented with arc lights in 1897 while filming the singer Paulus in his Robert-Houdin theatre, he did not install artificial lighting in his studios until around 1905, at which time he was alone among film-makers to do so. Until then, however, he was forced to film between the hours of eleven and three, when the sun was at its height. Once he had built his first studio in 1897, Méliès shot the vast majority of his films indoors, where he had more control over filming conditions. Rare scenes shot outdoors from this period include the parade of fantastical vehicles in *A la conquête du Pôle/ The Conquest of the Pole*, the triumphant return of the prince and princess in *Le Royaume des fées/The Kingdom of the Fairies* (1903), and the meeting in the town square between King Edward and President Fallières in *Le Tunnel sous la Manche/Tunnelling the English Channel* (1907).

Early cameras posed other challenges for film-makers. Extreme-ly heavy and unwieldy, they could not be moved easily, and certainly not while filming; the loud noise they made when shooting caused Méliès to refer to the camera as his *moulin à café*, or coffee grinder. Scenes, and thus entire films, were limited in length for several years by the camera's capacity to shoot only 20 metres of film at a time, which resulted in films with a running time of less than one minute. The depth and width of shots was more or less invariable, determined to a large extent by the camera lens used, as its focal length could not be adjusted or pulled. These constraints resulted in a static camera, forcing Méliès to create movement in shots by other means, including using movable sets, pulleys and cranes, and trap doors. The limited stage area (16 × 13 feet) caused problems for which Méliès came up with a number of solutions – with varying degrees of success. In the 1899 *Cendrillon/ Cinderella*, dancing couples crowd onto the dance floor at the ball, causing a perhaps unintentionally comic effect as they are forced to take baby steps. In the 1900 *Jeanne d'Arc/Joan of Arc*, courtiers and real horses parade across the stage from left to right, disappear into the wings, and circle round behind the stage to begin again from the left. In 1899, a narrow addition was built onto the first studio, which allowed the camera to be moved farther from the stage for the occasional long shot. The stage in Studio B, at about 30 feet wide, was double the width of the stage in the first studio, giving a different look to films made from the end of 1905 on.

As the orthochromatic filmstock available at the time distorted some colour values, Méliès painted sets, props and costumes in shades of grey, and had his actors wear black and white makeup. Although the Lumières had experimented with colour film (in fact, they showed colour still photographs along with their black-and-white films at the first film exhibitions in 1895, leading some observers to collapse the two media and 'remember' the moving pictures in colour), it had not been perfected, and was not available commercially. Nonetheless, most of Méliès's more elaborate *féeries* were sold *en couleurs*, laboriously hand painted by a team of women, headed by a Mme Thullier. The colouring was done frame by frame, and, although a labour-saving device known as a *pochoir*, which enabled twenty frames to be coloured at a time, was introduced by Pathé in 1903–04, Jacques Malthête, who has done the most extensive research on this subject, believes that Méliès used the device either very little or not at all (Malthête 1982: 159). Malthête's contention is supported by the fact that the blotches of colour in Méliès's films waver on the screen, sometimes leaping beyond the outlines of the image to which they have been applied, giving an artisanal feel to some of the films.

Early film was also subject to different projection conditions from those we experience today. Before the advent of permanent movie theatres, films in France were shown primarily at *fêtes foraines*, or fairgrounds, where cinema was just one attraction among many on an entertainment bill. Film projections varied greatly among exhibitors, who personalized them in a number of ways, including the speed at which they showed the films. Silent films were shot at a speed of fourteen to eighteen frames a second (although usually between sixteen and eighteen), compared to the modern speed of twenty-four frames a second. Consequently, silent films, when shown on television or in modern cinemas today, often appear speeded up and jerky, because they are being shown at a faster speed than that at which they were filmed. Exhibitors were at liberty to speed up or slow down films as they pleased when projecting them, even inverting the order of scenes in multi-scene films, or adding their own inserts. Méliès's use of dissolves from 1899 seems to have been, to a certain extent, a reaction to this practice, a way of gaining more authorial control. Abel points out that 'the dissolve seems to have had an important secondary function for Méliès – to restrict exhibitors from making alterations in the length and order of shots in the prints they purchased from him' (Abel 1998: 71).

The absence of sound, which was not introduced in French films until 1929–30, also allowed exhibitors a greater role in packaging the cinematic experience. Because intertitles were not in general use before 1902 or 1903 (and even after that, Méliès only used them very rarely), exhibitors employed a *bonimenteur*, or narrator, to tell the story or comment upon films as they were being shown, usually reading scripts provided by the production company, but sometimes using their own (see Malthête 1996a). Exhibitors also provided their own sound effects, which often included live music. As many film historians have noted, 'silent' films were anything but.

However, despite the contingencies of differing exhibition conditions, film-makers nonetheless wielded a certain amount of control over their work, both behind the camera and at the editing stage. Although many of Méliès's filmic special effects derived from the theatre (his first studio, as we have seen, was built to the exact dimensions of the Théâtre Robert-Houdin), he also used and developed a number of specifically cinematic techniques. The first and perhaps most frequently used *truc*, or special effect, in Méliès's repertoire – **substitution splicing** – created the sudden appearance or disappearance of a person or object, or the sudden replacement of one thing by another. The earliest surviving use of this technique occurs in *L'Escamotage d'une dame chez Robert Houdin/The Vanishing Lady* (1896), a classic magic act in which Méliès places a cloth over the seated Jehanne d'Alcy; when the cloth is removed, she is gone. Then, a skeleton suddenly appears in the place of the woman; Méliès covers the skeleton with the cloth, and when he removes it, the woman reappears. Méliès went on to use substitution splicing in most of his films, sometimes dozens of times within a very short period, as in *Les Illusions funambulesques/Extraordinary Illusions* (1903). For a long time, this technique was known as 'stop motion' (*arrêt de caméra*), a term that obscured its complexity. Jacques Malthête has pointed out that Méliès always filmed beyond the point where he planned to introduce the substitution, then cut the film at the appropriate place and spliced it very carefully – usually in the upper fourth or fifth of the frame – to the next piece of film containing the new image (Malthête 1996: 64–5). In light of Malthête's research, Alan Williams has suggested the term 'substitution splicing' as a more accurate reflection of Méliès's technique (Williams 1992: 36).

The story, often repeated by Méliès, of how he first came up with the idea of substitution splicing, is well known. While filming in front of the Opéra in Paris, his camera jammed; after fixing the problem, Méliès resumed filming. When he viewed the footage he had shot, he saw the omnibus he had been filming transform into a hearse, and men turn into women: the first cinematic *truc*, or special effect, was born. This tale of the apotheosis of the ordinary is, in all likelihood, apocryphal; it has been suggested that Méliès would probably have known about an earlier example of substitution splicing carried out by Thomas Edison in his 1895 *Execution of Mary Queen of Scots*, which Méliès would likely have shown at the Robert-Houdin (Deslandes & Richard 1968: 419). But the anecdote's apocryphal status only makes this filmic primal scene all the more compelling, its symbolism all the more insistent.

Paul Hammond points out that '[t]here is a distinction to be made between substituting an object for a counterfeit representation of itself (a dummy replacing Queen Mary on the scaffold) and changing one object into another quite different one. It is the difference between tautology and metaphor' (Hammond 1974: 35). Indeed, it is through metaphor that Méliès's work enters the realm of narrative. And Méliès's metaphors (the substitution of a hearse for an omnibus, or a woman for a man) are themselves symbolic. In the first case, Méliès pointed up the new medium's function as a kind of cenatograph, or writer of death; the transformation of an omnibus into a hearse suggests, more generally, the transformation of the living (of *all* living things, *omnibus*) in death. The very act of filming transforms the living into celluloid, which is then preserved, mummy-like, long after the living subject has died. Cinema, in other words, immortalizes the objects of its gaze. In the case of the transformation of men into women, the metamorphosis prefigured both the tranvestism that would pop up in many of Méliès's films, and the preoccupation with sexual difference (particularly in the form of the castration complex, since Méliès's anecdote tells of men turning into women) that would dominate film theory in the last three decades of the twentieth century.[3]

Méliès's bag of cinematic tricks included the following techniques, which quickly became the foundations of modern film-making:

Multiple exposure (*surimpression*) involved filming, recranking back to the point at which filming initially began, and then filming over the already exposed stock. Méliès used a metronome to make sure he turned the crank at a consistent speed, and then counted the number of times he turned the crank so as to go back over the same length of film when re-exposing it. This technique was used to produce several different effects, including dissolves, superimposition, what I will call a 'replication effect', and transparencies.

3 For cinema's preoccupation with death, see André Bazin on the 'mummy complex', or the cultural will to immortality in 'The Ontology of the Photographic Image' in Bazin 1984: 9–10; for discussions of the castration complex in film, see most works of Anglo-American film theory published in the last thirty years.

A **dissolve** is the superimposition of a fade-out onto a fade-in, achieved by reversing and then re-filming using film that has already been exposed once. Méliès first used this technique, which originated in magic lantern displays, in the 1899 *Cendrillon*, and then frequently thereafter to link scenes in multiple-shot films. From the beginning, the dissolve was usually not used for trick effect, but rather to create a smooth transition from one scene to the next.

A **matte shot** is a technique taken from still photography, in which part of the camera lens is covered so as to produce a blank spot; the film is then rewound and exposed again to record the image to be superimposed, but this time with everything blocked out except the area that had been covered before. This effect was also achieved by draping the area on which the object was to be superimposed in black cloth. Frazer notes that the technique was probably first used in film in 1897 by G. A. Smith of Brighton (76). A classic example, and one of the earliest, of Méliès's use of this technique can be seen in *Le Portrait mystérieux/The Mysterious Portrait* (1899), in which Méliès places a blank canvas inside a large, empty picture frame, sits beside it, and watches as an image of himself materializes on the canvas. The two Mélièses observe each other and converse.

Méliès used a **replication effect** (which he himself called a '*superposition*') in films such as *Le Mélomane/The Melomaniac* (1903), in which he throws his head onto telegraph wires shaped like a musical staff, and repeats the process several times, and in *L'Homme-orchestre/The One-Man Band* (1900), in which several Mélièses, each playing a different instrument, form a band. Méliès describes the precision involved in creating this effect in a text he wrote in 1906:

> The views performed by a single actor in which the film is successively exposed up to ten consecutive times in the camera, are so difficult that they become a veritable Chinese water torture. The actor, playing different scenes ten times, must remember precisely to the second, while the film is running, what he was doing at the same instant in earlier takes and the exact location where he was in the scene ... [I]f during one of the takes an actor makes an untoward gesture, if his arm moves in front of a

character photographed in the preceding take, it will be transparent and *out of focus* , which *wrecks* the trick [original emphasis]. You can see from this just how difficult it is and how angry you get when, after three or four hours of work and sustained attention, a tear rips through the film after the seventh or eighth superimposition, forcing you to abandon the film and do everything over again. (Abel 1988: 45)

The replication of Méliès's own image heralds the age of the simulacrum by suggesting, synecdochally, the mass mechanical reproduction of his work in both Britain and the United States – it is no accident that the bandleader's multiple heads in *Le Mélomane* form the musical notes to the tunes 'God Save the King' and 'America'.

To create a **transparency**, one image was recorded directly over another without blocking out the initial impression, resulting in a ghost-like effect, as in *Le Revenant/L'Apparition* (1903) and the skeletons' dance in *Le Palais des Mille et une nuits /The Palace of the Arabian Nights* (1905). Méliès used **model shots**, or miniature reproductions of outdoor locations, in several films, including the newsreel reconstruction *Éruption volcanique à la Martinique /The Eruption of Mount Pelée* (1902), and travel fantasies such as *Le Raid Paris-Monte Carlo en deux heures/An Adventurous Automobile Trip* (1905), when the automobile is shown gliding over hill and dale. They are used twice in *Le Voyage à travers l'impossible /The Impossible Voyage* (1904), when the train is shown winding around a hill in the background, and again when the fanciful trolley travels over the side of a mountain.

Many of the effects created today by means of camera movement were achieved by Méliès with a stationary camera. In *Faust aux enfers/The Damnation of Faust* (1903), Faust and Mephistopheles seem to be falling down an abyss, when they are actually dangling in front of a moving backdrop. A similar effect is created in *A la conquête du Pôle*, when the suffragette falls through the sky from a hot-air balloon. Méliès created a tracking effect by placing an object on rails and moving upward toward the stationary camera in a matte shot. In *L'Homme à la tête en caoutchouc/The Man with the Rubber Head* (1901), this technique is used to make

Méliès's head appear to grow larger until it explodes; in *Le Voyage dans la lune/A Trip to the Moon* (1902), the rocket appears to approach the moon. In a 1935 interview with Henri Langlois, founder of the Cinémathèque française, Méliès claims to have invented the close-up in *L'Homme à la tête en Caoutchouc*: 'Zecca a vainement cherché à reproduire ce trucage en approchant son appareil de la tête vissée; celle-ci débordait du plan de la table au fur et à mesure qu'elle grandissait. Je m'étais, au contraire, avancé vers l'appareil en me haussant petit à petit de façon à ce que mon menton restât dans le plan de la table. Je n'ai donc pas peur de dire que j'ai inventé le gros plan comme j'ai inventé les autres trucages'.[4]

But it was not only in his use of special effects that Méliès showed himself to be at the cutting edge of film technique. For example, Méliès occasionally used staging in depth, by having actors move along the camera axis, rather than restricting them to horizontal movement (depth of staging is not to be confused with depth of field or focus, which became more of an option once lenses were developed whose focus could be adjusted).[5] At least two scholars have noted that Méliès used staging in depth in two films in the *Affaire Dreyfus* series (1899), *Bagarre entre journalistes* and *Attentat contre Maître Labori* – despite (or perhaps because of) the fact that Noël Burch singles out *L'Affaire Dreyfus* as a classic example of 'primitive cinema' (Elsaesser 1990: 225).[6]

It is not widely known, however, that Méliès also used deep staging in the 1907 film *Le Tunnel sous la Manche/Tunnelling the English Channel* (when King Edward enters the frame in the scene

4 'Zecca sought in vain to reproduce this technique by moving the camera toward the head held in position; the head surpassed the plane of the table as it grew. I myself, on the other hand, approached the camera while rising slowly so that my chin remained on the same plane as that of the table. I therefore have no qualms about saying that I invented the close-up, just as I invented other special effects' (Langlois 1971: 43).

5 For a history of the use of staging in depth, see Bordwell, Chapter 6; Bordwell makes the distinction between depth of staging and depth of field at 158.

6 See Brewster, 'Deep Staging in French Films 1900-1914' in Elsaesser 1990: 45–55. (The dates in Brewster's title are misleading, given that Méliès's *'Affaire Dreyfus* was made in 1899.) See also Jenn (1984), who devotes considerable attention to these two films in the Dreyfus series.

shot outdoors); in the 1906 *Les Quat'cents farces du diable/The Merry Frolics of Satan* (when a man climbs onto a rooftop in the foreground and observes the scene of a train crash with his back to the camera); and in the 1904 films *Le Voyage à travers l'impossible / The Impossible Voyage* (as villagers in the foreground, with their backs to the camera, observe the wreckage of a trolley that has crashed into a building) and *Les Cartes vivantes/The Living Playing Cards* (when Méliès approaches the camera).

Additionally, Méliès also created edited sequences by breaking scenes down into several discrete shots, sometimes resulting in an effect of rapid montage, as in *Le Voyage dans la lune/A Trip to the Moon* (1902), in which the rocket's descent to Earth is shown in a four-shot sequence lasting two-and-a-half seconds. Méliès also used overlapping editing, in *Voyage dans la lune, Le Voyage à travers l'impossible* and *A la conquête du Pôle/Conquest of the Pole* (1912), in which the rocket, dirigible and airplane, respectively, are each shown landing twice from two different angles. Méliès began making multi-shot films linked either by cuts or by dissolves in 1899 (beginning with *Cendrillon*; the preceding film, *L'Affaire Dreyfus*, for many years considered by film historians to be Méliès's longest film to date, was actually a series of films sold together or individually).[7] Even Méliès's single-scene films (with the exception of the newsreel footage) are almost always composed of more than one shot, spliced together using the strictest continuity editing to achieve the illusion of a single take. This, after all, is the aesthetic that André Bazin was attempting to recuperate when he wrote that 'Essential cinema ... is to be found in straightforward photographic respect for the unity of space' (Bazin 1984: 46). Although Méliès broke temporal unity by cutting, he nonetheless preserved spatial unity through careful splicing, thereby preserving what Noël Burch calls the 'unicity of the frame' (cited in Abel 1998: 60).

Despite the advanced techniques and special effects outlined above, which eventually became the standard vocabulary of classical cinema, it is within the unicity of perspective, in his use of mise en scène, that Méliès made his greatest contribution to film history. He was able to tell stories within a single scene that most other

7 See Malthête 1981: 70.

film-makers needed dozens or hundreds to tell. Yet, as we have seen, the narrative element of his work has often been overlooked in discussions of its spectacular dimension. Therefore, in what follows, individual scenes of some of his films will be examined using a model of structural analysis designed for narrative films.

La Grande Paradigmatique: Méliès and Metz

Film scholars have long hesitated to bring the concepts of contemporary – or even what is, by now, quite dated – film theory to bear on the earliest films, as if films before Griffith and theory after Bazin were separated by an unbreachable divide, summed up in Noël Burch's designation of early cinema as a 'primitive otherness' (Burch 1990: 198). More recently, André Gaudreault has characterized Méliès's films as 'irreductiblement étranger au cinéma qui l'a suivi'.[8] But by examining Méliès's films in the light of a structural model of narrative analysis designed with modern films in mind, we can begin to erode the entirely artificial dichotomy between early and modern cinema. Christian Metz developed the *grande syntagmatique* in order to break film down into discrete units of meaning, each of which could be analyzed in relation to the whole film. He elaborated this model in the mid 1960s, when structuralism was at its height. By transposing the semiotic analysis of the smallest units of meaning from written language to film, Metz sought to identify a 'cinematic grammar' (Metz 1974: 179). The question underlying this model was: 'How does film constitute itself as a narrative discourse?' (Stam *et al.* 1992: 38).

It should be noted that to invoke Metz as a way of demonstrating narrative complexity in Méliès is to pit Metz against himself, for Metz locates what he calls '[t]he merging of the cinema and of narrativity' (Metz 1974: 93) at around 1915, with the production of D. W. Griffith's *Birth of a Nation*. For Metz, as for many other film scholars, this film marked a turning point in the history of cinema: 'Thus, it was in a single motion that the cinema

8 'irreducibly foreign with regard to the cinema that followed it' (Gaudreault in Malthête and Marie 1997: 112).

became narrative and took over some of the attributes of a language' (Metz 1974: 96). Yet, just a few lines earlier, Metz had written that Méliès had 'wanted above all to tell a story' (95). So, while he accords Méliès's work a storytelling function, Metz denies the earliest film a 'coherent syntax' (95). In what follows, however, it will become apparent that film and narrative did not need to 'merge', because narrative syntax was present within film from the beginning. Without denying the evolution of editing techniques that occurred throughout the silent era, it is still possible to locate in early film the narrative functions that Metz identifies in film of the later period. In extending Metz's *grande syntagmatique* to the early period, the point is not to universalize Metz's model, but rather to demonstrate the shared kinship between Méliès's work and later modes of filmic representation. The aim of such an application is to show the debt that modern cinema owes to Méliès – not just in spirit, but in structural complexity as well.

However, instead of analyzing Méliès's films in units of scenes or shots, which is often precluded by many of the earliest films' single-shot structure, it is possible to locate interpretive units at another level, within rather than between *tableaux* or scenes. If syntagmas are the diachronic (or temporally determined) units of sequential progression, then we may call *paradigmas* the synchronic (or spatially determined) units of meaning that coexist within a single tableau, at the level of the mise en scène.[9] We can thus transpose many of Metz's observations about inserts and multiple-shot sequences to Méliès's single-shot films, and to individual sequence shots within longer, multi-shot films. That the unicity of the frame, or spatially unbroken *tableau*, is considered to be a defining characteristic of the cinema of attractions is all the more compelling a reason to focus on it as a testing ground for the hypothesis of narrative coherence in very early cinema – yet, as we shall see, the very features that characterize unicity of the frame are those that link early cinema to later

9 My use of the word 'paradigma' should not be confused with Metz's use of the term 'paradigm', by which he designates a film-maker's selection of a particular syntagma over others. See Rosen 1986: 45–53.

cinema.[10] For the purposes of a paradigmatic analysis, discrete units of meaning will thus be examined primarily in their spatial, as opposed to strictly temporal, context. The question, in other words, is the extent to which Méliès's use of mise en scène fulfils a narrative function. What aspects of a story, which normally unfold through time, may be conveyed spatially? Gunning argues that '[e]arly films are enframed rather than emplotted' (Elsaesser 1990: 101); my contention is that it is precisely their enframing that gives rise to early films' emplotment.

In order to conduct an analysis of this kind, it will be necessary to collapse Metz's basic distinction between the autonomous shot and the multi-shot syntagma. Disregarding this distinction, however, is not as dismissive a gesture as it might appear, because the distinction was questioned by Metz himself: 'Combinations that avoid *collage*-juxtaposition (i.e., continuity shooting, long shots, sequence shots, using the resources of the "wide screen," and so on) are nonetheless ... examples of montage in the broad sense' (Rosen 1986: 51; original emphasis). Méliès used most of the techniques mentioned by Metz – not all of which could be expected to occur in any single film (Metz 1974: 179) – to achieve complexity within a shot, or 'montage' without editing. It is this complexity that will now be considered, in an examination of individual tableaux in the context of the eight elements of Metz's *grande syntagmatique*.

Insert

An insert effect is achieved paradigmatically by Méliès in shots that include images that are at once self-contained (usually framed in some way) and part of the larger scene. In Méliès's prototype of the insert, the alternative view shares the frame with the 'main' subject, instead of alternating with it as later inserts do. This boxing effect was achieved either cinematically, through editing

---

10 As Bordwell suggests, 'If we are concentrating on staging and its corollary problems of directing attention, we may not need to distinguish between the cinema of attractions and what followed' (1997: 268).

(matte shots), or theatrically, by building a small stage-within-a-stage. Matte shots were the most common of these techniques. In *Le Portrait mystérieux/The Mysterious Portrait* (1899), Méliès conducts a conversation with a life-sized portrait of himself, which has been superimposed onto a black space in a picture frame through multiple exposure of the filmstock. (Méliès later developed a technique for producing matte shots on a white background, of which he boasted – in both French and English – in the 1903 *Le Portrait spirite/A Spiritualist Photographer*: 'Spiritualistic photo Dissolving effect obtained without black background GREAT NOVELTY'). He also varied the size of the superimposed object: in the 1903 *L'Enchanteur Alcofribas/Alcofribas, the Master Magician*, a close-up of Jehanne d'Alcy's head is made to float in the air, while in the 1901 *L'Homme à la tête en caoutchouc/The Man with the Rubber Head* and the 1902 *Voyage dans la lune*, Méliès's head and the moon appear, respectively, to grow or approach by means of the inverted tracking technique that Méliès invented (which Abel (1998: 63) describes as 'the illusion of a dolly shot'), in which an object was pushed up a ramp toward the immobile camera, giving the impression that the camera was approaching the object.

The theatrical alternative to the matte shot, the stage-within-a-stage technique, was less commonly used. In *Les Hallucinations du Baron de Munchausen/Baron Munchausen's Dream* (1911), terrifying dream images, including a huge spider-woman, devils and a winged dragon, appear above the baron's bed, with the actors actually perched on a small platform built onto the set. Similarly, in *Le Sorcier/The Witch's Revenge* (1903), a wizard makes the Three Graces appear on a little stage that has been brought in for the purpose. Occasionally, both a matte shot and the stage-within-a-stage technique were used within a single scene, as in the 1906 *Les Affiches en goguette/The Hilarious Posters,* in which the Tripolin poster alternately shows three men squashed into a wooden square, and a superimposed shot of the men running around within the square, reduced in size.[11]

11 This would be the difference, to use an analogy from American television contemporary with Metz's analysis, between *Hollywood Squares* and the opening credits of *The Brady Bunch*.

There are three kinds of **non-diegetic insert** in Méliès's films, all of which interrupt the narrative. The first kind of insert effect occurs when characters bow to the audience at the end of a magic trick; this can be seen more often in the earlier films, such as *Escamotage d'une dame/The Vanishing Lady* (1896). A second kind of insert effect is achieved when there is a dance sequence in the middle of a scene that does not advance the narrative, as in *La Lanterne magique/The Magic Lantern* (1903), where the troupe of ballerinas spring out of the projector and dance around in a ring, or *Faust aux enfers/The Damnation of Faust* (1903), when a troupe of ballerinas perform for the camera. Finally, this effect may take the form of a spectacular tableau at the end of the film – what Burch calls an 'apothéose' (Elsaesser 1990: 222) – when the main characters are shown posing together as if for a group photo, often presided over by a brightly illuminated fairy, as at the end of *Cendrillon/Cinderella* (1899) and *Barbe-bleue/Blue-beard* (1901), or, conversely, by a bat-winged Mephistopheles, as in *Faust aux enfers/The Damnation of Faust* (1903).[12] These non-diegetic inserts certainly qualify as features of a 'cinema of attractions', but they are only one aspect of a much larger body of techniques, and cannot adequately encapsulate Méliès's entire *oeuvre*, let alone individual films in their entirety. These would be the moments that Mulvey designates as 'spectacle', which both disrupt and enhance the narrative while providing visual pleasure.

The **subjective insert**, in both Metz and Méliès, is an image seen in a dream or hallucination, visible to a particular character but not to others actually or potentially present. The frightening figures that hover over the baron's bed in *Les Hallucinations du Baron de Munchausen* would fit this description, as would the ghosts and dancing keys that torment the guilt-stricken wife as

12 It should be noted that this film, which features inventive special effects including a tilt shot showing Mephistopheles and Faust descending into hell and a series of transparencies superimposed on a waterfall, is sometimes confused with *La Damnation du docteur Faust/Faust and Marguerite* (1904), a much less dynamic film using operatic staging and uncharacteristically long shots, made the following year. This confusion probably arises from the resemblance between the English title of the earlier film (*The Damnation of Faust*) and the French title of the later film (*La Damnation du docteur Faust*).

she attempts to sleep in *Barbe-bleue*. Similarly, in *Le Rêve de l'horloger/The Clockmaker's Dream* (1904) a clockmaker dreams that his clocks are transformed into young women in seductive poses. In all three films, the inserts represent figments of the characters' imaginations.

For Metz, an **explanatory insert** is a shot that clarifies a plot point, such as a close-up of a murder weapon or the face of the murderer if as yet unknown to the other characters. Méliès uses enlarged props to draw attention to objects that might otherwise be difficult to notice. In *Barbe-bleue*, the key to the forbidden room and the champagne bottle are both unnaturally big, as is the key that the devil brandishes in the 1902 *Le Trésor de Satan/The Treasures of Satan*. The exaggerated size of these props makes them visible when they might be dwarfed by the set if they were of normal size. Similarly, in *Les Cartes vivantes/The Living Playing Cards* (1904) Méliès approaches the camera while holding up a playing card so that both the (non-diegetic) film audience and the (diegetic) theatrical audience can make out its suit. A form of explanatory insert is also achieved any time a magician (always played by Méliès) passes his hand through or under something to show the audience that there is 'nothing up his sleeve' (as, again, in *Les Cartes vivantes*, when Méliès taps and stomps on a bench in order to demonstrate its solidity, or when, in the 1904 *Thaumaturge chinois/Tchin-Chao, the Chinese Conjurer*, he turns the large box to the camera to show that it is empty). In the middle of a description of *Un Homme de tête/Four Troublesome Heads* (1898), Méliès wrote: 'Pour montrer qu'il n'y a aucune illusion dans ces trucs, [le prestidigitateur] passe sous la table sur laquelle est posée sa première tête' (cited in Sadoul 1970: 118).[13] An explanatory insert would also include the use of any expository or anticipatory gestures to the audience, as when the magician circles his hand around his face to announce that we are about to see a likeness of himself or another person appear, as in *Le Portrait mystérieux/The Mysterious Portrait* (1899) and *Le Portrait spirite/A Spiritualist Photographer* (1903).

13 'To show that no trickery is involved in these illusions, the magician passes beneath the table on which the first head is sitting'.

A **displaced diegetic insert** is a shot (or sequence) that is temporally or spatially displaced. In Méliès, examples of such an insert would include the close-up of the woman's face in *L'Enchanteur Alcofribas/Alcofribas, the Master Magician* (1903), the waterfall scene in *Faust aux enfers/The Damnation of Faust* (1903), and the projected images (superimpositions) in *La Lanterne magique/The Magic Lantern* (1903). Unlike subjective inserts, displaced diegetic inserts are meant to be objectively present. For example, it is possible to distinguish between *Faust aux enfers*, in which Faust is shown the waterfall with superimposed images of people in it, and *Les Hallucinations du Baron de Munchausen*. In the first case, the superimposition is objective in the sense that we are meant to believe that these figures are actually appearing in the waterfall; in the second case, the superimposition is subjective because we are not meant to believe that the figures are actually hovering above the Baron's bed, but rather that they are appearing to him in a dream. Subjective inserts belong to the realm of the fantastic, as elaborated by Tzvetan Todorov (1975), which is characterized by a moment of hesitation, in which both character and viewers wonder whether what they are experiencing is real or imagined. The displaced diegetic insert in Méliès, on the other hand, is a function of the marvellous, a fictional world that operates on entirely different rules from those that govern our own.

Parallel syntagma

The paradigmatic version of the parallel syntagma, or cross-cutting between scenes that would not normally be associated, is symbolic substitution splicing. In each case, two different subjects are shown in succession. Although not normally linked temporally or spatially, they are spliced together in the film to form a thematic or symbolic link. Metz gives as examples 'scenes of the life of the rich interwoven with scenes of the life of the poor, images of tranquility alternating with images of disturbance, shots of the city and of the country, of the sea and of wheat fields' (Rosen 1986: 47). Although three of these pairs are opposites (with the fourth constituting, arguably, a difference rather than an opposition), they are all posited as structural equivalents. It is conceivable that most, or even all, of Méliès's substitutions could be shown to convey symbolic equivalence, but here the focus will be limited to the overtly symbolic instances.

Méliès created a variety of symbolic substitutions (e.g., women turning into butterflies in the 1906 *Bulles de savon animées/Soap Bubbles*, suggesting an equivalence between women and these fragile, unthreatening objects of beauty; or, in *Illusions fantas-magoriques/The Famous Box Trick* (1898), one little boy becoming two little boys who squabble and tussle before being transformed into the British and United States flags, evoking the American War of Independence). But the majority of Méliès's symbolic substitutions are informed by the two foundational metamor-phoses displayed in the filmic primal scene in front of the Opéra: death (the substitution of a hearse for an omnibus) and the transformation of genders.

Many of the films that invoke death do so unambiguously. Jehanne d'Alcy's metamorphosis into a skeleton in *Escamotage d'une dame chez Robert-Houdin* is a kind of *memento mori*, remind-ing viewers that this is the way of all flesh. *Le Monstre/The Monster* (1903) also depicts a transformation from youthful, flesh-and-blood woman to skeleton (though within a sequence that is the exact opposite of that in *Escamotage*: *Le Monstre* begins with a skeleton, which is brought to life, only to be turned back into a skeleton). Films that show people (almost always women) being turned into a shower of shredded paper, feathers, or clothing also fall into the category of the *memento mori* film, which represents the disinte-gration of the inanimate body associated with death. Examples of this include *Illusions funambulesques/Extraordinary Illusions* (1903), in which a woman turns into shredded paper and a lifeless bundle of clothing, and *L'Impressionniste fin-de-siècle /An Up-to-date Conjurer* (1899), in which a woman is turned into a cascade of feathers.

The fact that the vast majority of these *memento mori* films use women as their object links them to the other most common form of symbolic substitution, the switching of genders. The transform-ation of men into women enacts the castration scenario (as in the

1898 films *Le Magicien/The Magician*, in which the male magician turns into a female dancer in mid-air, and, most spectacularly, *La Tentation de Saint-Antoine/The Temptation of St Anthony*, in which Christ on the cross turns into a female seductress), while the transformation of women into men reassuringly reverses this scenario, though more often through transvestism than through substitution splicing: Méliès's films abound in women dressed as male sailors, courtiers, pages, etc. It is worth noting that the men who turn into women are almost invariably transformed back into men, whereas the cross-dressing women rarely shed their male-signifying clothing (an exception is the 1908 *Le Tambourin fantastique/The Knight of the Black Art*, in which the apparently male pages assisting the medieval magician are revealed near the end of the film to have been women 'all along'; to emphasize the point, the magician throws dresses on them).[14]

Richard Abel has noted that the *vue à transformations* was the dominant film style at the turn of the century, and that Méliès was its chief practitioner (Abel 1998: 61). The emphasis on transformation in early cinema is continued in modern-day Hollywood narratives, which, in some ways, are distended versions of the *vue à transformations*. The classic Hollywood film – or, for that matter, television – script requires the protagonist to learn and 'grow'; in other words, to undergo a transformation. He or she must usually (pick one): (a) become more caring and altruistic; (b) stop and smell the roses; (c) make a romantic commitment; (d) learn to trust others; (e) generally see the error of her or his ways; (f) gain self-confidence and poise; or (g) all of the above. Méliès's films feature similar transformations, but telescoped in time; and, because of the (necessary) emphasis placed on the visual in silent film, the transformations tended to be physical rather than psychological (although many Hollywood transformations, too, are primarily physical, or at least conveyed physically: ugly duckling into swan, child into adult, bookish boy into muscular conqueror).

14 John Frazer (1979: 188) does not mention this aspect of the film in his synopsis of the plot.

The difference between substitution splicing and Metz's parallel syntagma is that, in substitution, the subjects occupy exactly the same diegetic space, while in parallel montage they do not. In both techniques, an impression of structural equivalence, or parallelism between the two subjects shown in succession, is conveyed: either the subjects are performing a comparable (or opposing) activity, or they are themselves posited as interchangeable. This structural equivalence has a poetic value, like any trope; as Roman Jakobson said of poetry, filmic substitution collapses the poles of the syntagmatic (or the metonymic, metonymy being the figure of succession, by means of which Metz described the primary structure of cinema, its movement) and the paradigmatic, or metaphorical (the substitution of one thing for another).[15] Méliès's use of filmic substitution is metaphor in motion.

Bracket syntagma

The bracket syntagma depicts 'typical' examples of a certain activity, with no temporal sequence (or spatial coherence). The same character(s) may be shown repeating similar activities on different occasions: Metz gives the example of 'the first erotic images of *Une Femme mariée* (Jean-Luc Godard, 1964) [that] sketch a global picture of "modern love" through variations and partial repetitions' (Rosen 1986: 47). In Méliès, a **bracket paradigma** would result from replication, achieved through a patient use of multiple exposure: in each case, two different subjects are shown in succession which, although not necessarily linked temporally or spatially, are identifiable with each other. Just as in Metz's bracket syntagma, two subjects that could not normally be linked temporally and spatially – in the case of *L'Homme-orchestre/The One-Man Band* (1900), it would be physically impossible for one man to be in several spots, performing several distinct activities, at the same time – are brought together on the screen by means of

15 '*The poetic function projects the principle of equivalence from the axis of selection into the axis of combination.* Equivalence is promoted to the constitutive device of the sequence.' (Jakobson 1990: 78; original emphasis.)

editing. With the 'replication effect', Méliès anticipates cubism by showing the same subject from several different perspectives at once.[16]

Descriptive syntagma

The descriptive syntagma is basically an establishing shot, in which the camera lingers on a scene in order to allow viewers to situate themselves before a particular event takes place. (To use a grammatical analogy, the descriptive syntagma would be the continuous action or filmic *imparfait* that is interrupted by the *passé composé* or intervening event.) In Méliès, the **descriptive paradigma** applies to moments such as the market scene in *Le Raid Paris-Monte Carlo/An Adventurous Automobile Trip* (1905), in which villagers are shown going about their shopping before the king's car ploughs into the stalls; or the colloquium of learned men convening at the beginning of *Voyage dans la lune* or *A la conquête du Pôle*; or the banquet scene at the beginning of *Le Voyage à travers l'impossible*, at which the inventor of the fantastical vehicles displays his plans to potential investors. The descriptive paradigma may also be located in a film such as *Le Rêve de l'horloger/The Clockmaker's Dream* (1904), in which the clock-maker settles into his chair before nodding off and dreaming. All the dream films would fit this pattern, because they do not launch right into the dream but first establish the presence of the 'reality' that lets us know that the dream is 'only' a dream.

Alternating syntagma

Metz's alternating syntagma (cross-cutting between two elements of a single event, such as pursuer and pursued in a chase scene, to show simultaneity) appears in paradigmatic form in many of Méliès's films. The **alternating paradigma** involves the use of

16 See John Frazer, 'Le cubisme et le cinéma de Georges Méliès', in Malthête-Méliès 1984: 157–67.

multiple sites of action, such as foreground/background, upper/ lower, or left/right, within the frame. A foreground/background division occurs in the 1903 *Le Royaume des fées/Kingdom of the Fairies*, as the ghostly convoy gallops up into the sky while the prince and court look on in horror from the palace balcony, and in *Le Voyage dans la lune*, when the celestial creatures converse in the upper half of the frame while the exhausted interplanetary explorers sleep below them on the surface of the moon. *Le Tunnel sous la Manche/Tunnelling the English Channel* (1907) uses the illusion of a frame split vertically down the middle, an effect achieved profilmically rather than by editing, in order to show both the King of the British Isles and the President of France settling into bed (Méliès plays with this illusion by having the French President cross the wall and enter the King's bedroom, in England). All of the aforementioned effects are derived from the theatre. However, in *Le Royaume des fées*, there is also another depiction of simultaneity – a 'meanwhile' effect – in the form of a superimposed dissolve to the castle where the princess is being held prisoner, which the witch shows to the prince at his father's palace.

Scene

The scene is basically the same in Méliès, but his use of continuity editing was much more spatially focused that that of most other film-makers, to the extent that it may more accurately be called 'unicity editing'. According to Metz, '[t]he signifier is fragmentary in the scene – a number of shots, all of them only partial "profiles" (*Abschattungen*) – but the signified is unified and continuous' (Rosen 1986: 49). Almost all of Méliès's scenes contain effects (substitution, multiple exposure, etc.) that entail the splicing together of at least two shots, but whereas later film-makers would strive for variety in their shots, Méliès aimed for such precise continuity of angle and position within the frame that he created the illusion of unicity. Only the earliest films, such as *Une partie de cartes /A Game of Cards* and *Une nuit terrible/A Terrible Night* (both

1896), and the unstaged films such as *Panorama pris d'un train en marche/Panorama from the Top of a Moving Train* (1898), are composed of a single, continuous take.

Episodic sequence

An episodic sequence shows select occasions across time, to represent development. Metz gives the example of the breakfast scene in *Citizen Kane*, which condenses the gradual disintegration of Kane's first marriage into a few seconds (Rosen 1986: 50)

Examples of episodic sequences in Méliès can be found in *Les Cartes vivantes/The Living Playing Cards* (1904), in which the card grows bigger and bigger in three stages, the 1899 *Cendrillon/ Cinderella*, in which a pumpkin turns progressively into a coach and mice grow into footmen, and *Barbe-bleue/Blue-beard* (1901), in which the key grows in stages when Barbe-bleue's new wife is in the secret room (as distinct from an earlier scene, in which she is first presented with the larger-than-life keys). To be sure, Méliès's episodic sequences tend to cover a much smaller segment of time than those described by Metz. An episodic sequence would be distinct from reverse tracking shots (as in *L'Homme à la tête de caoutchouc/The Man with the Rubber Head*), or magnification through close framing (as in *Voyage dans la lune*), because in the latter two cases, no impression of stages or episodes is conveyed.

Ordinary sequence

The ordinary sequence skips unnecessary detail; in Méliès, this would include any scene that shows something done faster and more efficiently than it actually would be. Examples include the throwing of the clothes on and off a woman in *Illusions funambulesques/Extraordinary Illusions* (1903) and *Le Portrait spirite/A Spiritualist Photographer* (1903); throwing paintings onto a wall in *Le Locataire diabolique/The Diabolic Tenant* (1910); erecting the large picture frame in *Le Portrait mystérieux/The Mysterious*

Portrait (1899), and drawing a face more rapidly than is physically possible in *Le Roi du maquillage/Untamable Whiskers* (1904). The effect of accelerated motion was achieved by advancing the film more slowly than usual, so that when it was shown at normal speed the action appeared faster than normal. Sometimes, an entire film may be composed of an ordinary sequence, as the 1902 *Sacre d'Edouard VII/Coronation of King Edward VII*, which, as André Gaudreault points out, 'reconstitue en un seul plan apparent d'une durée très limitée un événement cérémonieux qui aurait pu durer (et a effectivement duré) beaucoup plus long-temps' (Gaudreault 1988: 21–2 n. 11).[17]

This chapter began with a discussion of the ways in which Méliès transformed theatrical techniques into cinematic effects, and proceded to a demonstration of the narrative function of Méliès's use of staging. This progression is a natural one, considering that filmic mise en scène, as the word *scène*, or stage, indicates, derives from the theatre. By mapping Metz's syntagmas on to Méliès's tableaux, it is possible to demonstrate the modernity of Méliès's work, its structural affinity with films we might see today; but it is equally possible to demonstrate the extent to which film borrows from the traditional art of the theatre, and, through the use of cinematic techniques, makes it new. Narrative is the thread that links Méliès's films both to the arts that preceded (and, to some extent, engendered) them and to the body of cinematic work that followed them.

   Obviously, it is important not to lose sight of a film's historical specificity, and not to reduce it to a mere confirmation of the supposed 'universality' of a theory penned decades later, a gesture that would dehistoricize both film and theory. Nor is it the idea to 'see the primitive cinema as a lost paradise and to fail to see the emergence of the IMR [Institutional Mode of Representation, or set of pictorial conventions developed after 1906–07] as an objective advance', as Burch rightly criticizes other historians for doing (Burch 1990: 198). But in using the tools of modern

17 'reconstitutes in a single visible shot of a very limited duration a ceremonial event that could have lasted (and did, in fact, last) much longer'.

analysis to examine early cinema, we can show the extent to which these films influenced later work on which modern film theory tests its hypotheses. The goal of such an exercise is to contribute to a model of film history based on a continuous tension between narrative and spectacle, rather than on a series of mutually exclusive epistemological breaks.

Like the shift in emphasis from diachronic to synchronic study that I have proposed here, it would be fruitful to cultivate an analogous shift from an emphasis on history to an emphasis on filmic analysis in the context of early cinema. There is no need to consign early films to the exclusive domain of the film historian, who documents developments *between* films, rather than within them. It is no longer possible to imagine that films made before a certain period do not lend themselves to the same analytical rigour as films made more recently. Méliès's work must be reassessed in its own right, and in the light of its influence on film-makers who followed in his footsteps. In the following chapters, I will examine generic and thematic aspects of Méliès's work, in an attempt to illustrate further its narrative and symbolic force.

References

Abel, R. (1988), *French Film Theory and Criticism 1907–1939*, vols. I and II, Princeton, NJ, Princeton University Press.

—— (1998), *The Ciné Goes to Town*, Berkeley, CA, University of California Press.

Bazin, A. (1984), *What is Cinema?* vol. I, trans. Hugh Gray, Berkeley, CA, University of California Press.

Benjamin, W. (1978), *Reflections*, trans. Edmund Jephcott, New York, Harcourt Brace Jovanovich.

Bordwell, D. (1997), *On the History of Film Style*, Cambridge, MA, Harvard University Press.

Burch, N. (1990), *Life to Those Shadows*, trans. and ed. Ben Brewster, London, BFI.

Deslandes, J. and Richard, J. (1968), *Histoire comparée du cinéma* vol. II (Belgium?), Casterman.

Elsaesser, T. (ed.) (1990), *Early Cinema: Space, Frame, Narrative*, London, British Film Institute.

Frazer, J. (1979), *Artificially Arranged Scenes*, Boston, G. K. Hall & Company.

Gaudreault, A. (1988), *Du littéraire au filmique* (n.d.), Les Presses de l'Université Laval, Méridiens Klincksieck.

Hammond, P. (1974), *Marvellous Méliès*, London, Gordon Fraser.

Jakobson, R. (1990), *On Language*, ed. Linda R. Waugh and Monville-Burston, M., Cambridge, MA, Harvard University Press.

Langlois, H. (1971), 'Georges Méliès, magicien du cinéma', *Cinema* 152, jan.

Malthête, J. (1981), *Essai de Reconstitution du catalogue français de la Star-Film*, (?), Centre Nationale de la Cinématographie.

—— (1982), 'Couleurs, coloris et colorants des "Star" films', *Les Cahiers de la Cinémathèque* 35/36, 156–9.

—— (1996), *Méliès, images et illusions*, Paris, Exporégie.

—— (1996a), 'Méliès et le conférencier', *Iris* 22, Autumn.

Malthête, J. and Marie, M. (eds) (1997), *Georges Méliès l'illusionniste fin de siècle?* Paris, Presses de la Sorbonne Nouvelle.

Malthête-Méliès, M (ed.) (1984), *Méliès et la naissance du spectacle cinématographique*, (Paris), Klincksieck.

Metz, Christian (1974), *Film Language: A Semiotics of the Cinema*, trans. Michael Taylor, Chicago, University of Chicago Press.

Rosen, P. (1986), *Narrative, Apparatus, Ideology*, New York, Columbia University Press.

Sadoul, G. (1947) 'Georges Méliès et la première élaboration du langage cinématographique', *Revue Internationale de la Filmologie* 1, juillet–août, 23–30.

—— (1970), *Georges Méliès*, Paris, Seghers.

Stam, Robert *et al.* (eds) (1992), *New Vocabularies in Film Semiotics*, London, Routledge.

Williams, A. (1992), *Republic of Images: A History of French Filmmaking*, Cambridge, MA, Harvard University Press.

2

Fantastic realism

Méliès has traditionally been associated with fantasy and illusion, as the titles of several books in English on the filmmaker suggest (*Artificially Arranged Scenes*; *Marvellous Méliès*; *Méliès, Father of Film Fantasy*). The association of Méliès with fantasy is due in large part to the selection of films shown at the Salle Pleyel during the 1929 gala evening in Méliès's honour, which (re)introduced Méliès's work to a new generation of film enthusiasts. The programme was composed of recently rediscovered films that had been commissioned by the Dufayel Department Store (see p. 19). Naturally, these films were all *féeries* and other child-friendly subjects, giving the misleading impression that this kind of film was the most representative of Méliès's work.

In fact, as we have seen, Méliès worked in all genres, and took pride in the realistic aspects of even his most fantastical films, as this description of the thirteenth tableau from *Le Royaume des fées/ The Kingdom of the Fairies* (1903) in the English edition of the Star-Film catalogue suggests:

> Encountering a Tempest at Sea: this tableau is one of the cleverest arrangements for cinematographs. The sea is represented with striking fidelity to nature by natural water agitated mechanically. The rain is likewise obtained by the use of real water. The movement of the clouds and the lightning are rendered with such striking vividness that the tableau has a marvellous appearance of reality.

Méliès's description of tableau 15, however, gently mocks the pretence to realism that his synopsis of the earlier tableau had displayed: 'Sinking to the Bottom of the Sea. (Real Fishes and Sea Monsters)' (Sadoul (ed.) 1947: 19).

While it is true that most of Méliès's films exhibit an element of the marvellous – evidence of this is scattered throughout this study – many of them call into question the very distinction between fantasy and reality. As a magician, Méliès was a master of illusion; in his films, he often played with the boundaries between reality and representation, fact and fantasy. Méliès's stage illusions had caused spectators to question their own grasp of reality: what they saw before them appeared to be real, yet it was clearly not so. Similarly, several of his films highlight the illusory nature of the realist aesthetic of mimesis. This chapter will consider Méliès's treatment of the relationship between fantasy and realism, first by examining a selection of films that explicitly thematize representation, and then by discussing several of the *actualités reconstitutées*, or filmic reconstructions of actual events.

The realist illusion

Perhaps the earliest of Méliès's films to foreground the relation between realistic representation and artifice is *Le Portrait mystérieux/The Mysterious Portrait* (1899). When the film opens, we see a bourgeois interior showing a double door flanked by two framed portraits of a man and a woman, half of a bookshelf, a poster with the words 'PASSEZ MUSCADES' written on it, and two posters in the style of popular graphic artist Jules Chéret advertising the Robert-Houdin theatre (Frazer incorrectly describes the decor as a 'painted backdrop of a pastoral scene' (1979: 75)). A huge gilt picture frame stands in the centre. Méliès enters, throws off the straw hat he is wearing (uncharacteristically), walks in front of the frame, and outlines the shape of a rectangle with his hands.[1]

---

1 Perhaps the only other surviving film in which Méliès appears wearing a straw hat is the first one he ever made, *Une partie de cartes/Playing Cards* (1896), a remake of the Lumières' *Une partie d'écarté* (1895).

He then walks behind the frame and steps through it, bowing while within it. The backdrop depicting the bourgeois interior behind him rolls up to reveal another backdrop depicting a medieval exterior (a river with bridge, a boat, buildings). Méliès fetches a large painted canvas depicting a tree-filled countryside and inserts it in the gilt frame. He places a stool in the frame, kneels beside the painting, and waves his hand around his face in a circle – a gestural code from theatrical magic that will be repeated in many of his films. He 'zaps' the painting with his hand and it turns into a very blurred photographic image (suggestive of an Impressionist painting), which gradually focuses to reveal Méliès himself sitting on the stool. The first Méliès, to the right of the frame, performs the same circular gesture around his face again. The Méliès in the frame leans over and congratulates his look-alike by shaking his own hands together, but then makes fun of his creator by pointing to his own bald head and laughing. The first Méliès, angered, 'zaps' the framed image, which gradually blurs and fades to black.

From the first moments of this film, the posters advertising the Robert-Houdin theatre provide a self-referential wink to the film audience. They also point up the relationship between the media of theatre and film, both in general – film was viewed by many as an extension of the theatre – and within this particular film (in the blend of theatrical effects, such as the double backdrop, and cinematic effects, such as the use of variable focus and a matte shot). The transformation of the painted canvas into a photographic image is a representation in microcosm of the historical transition from painting to photography as the dominant mode of visual representation; it is no accident that this transition is signalled by a cinematic device, as film would ultimately overtake both other media in cultural impact.

The expression 'Passez Muscades' on one of the posters (which can be translated as 'taa-daa' or 'hey presto') functions on two levels: it evokes the magic acts performed at the Robert-Houdin theatre, and it also alerts film viewers that a trick is being played on them. When Méliès steps through the picture frame, he is performing a typical magician's gesture that will help the audience suspend its disbelief by demonstrating that the frame is indeed truly hollow. Similarly, when he puts the canvas in the frame, he is first of all doing a magic trick, making us believe that there are no false compartments or strings attached to the canvas because we have witnessed its construction; but at the same time he is saying something about the construction of mimetic representation itself. His gesture emphasizes the constructed, or artificial, nature of meaning, by suggesting that pictures must be placed in frames, that referents must be attached to signs created by convention if they are to acquire significance. Artifice is also thematized in the double backdrops, a *mise en abîme* that plays on our expectations about the theatrical unmasking: what lies behind the theatrical, Méliès is suggesting, is another mask. The double-backdrop effect is also a prototype of the multi-scene film, which Méliès first produced later that year (*Cendrillon*); here, he uses a theatrical device to achieve an effect that would later be created in the editing room.

This film also offers a metaphor for Méliès's dual role as both filmmaker and actor, in the form of the artist who doubles as his own subject: here, the *sujet de l'énonciation* (the speaker, or anyone who creates meaning, such as an artist) merges with the *sujet de l'énoncé* (that which is being said, or that which is depicted, such as the man shown in the portrait), a doubling that will reappear in *Les Cartes vivantes*, discussed below, in which a magician brings an image to life, and then reveals that the creature he has brought to life is none other than himself.

Like *Le Portrait mystérieux*, *Le Portrait spirite/A Spiritualist photographer* (1903) refers to a representational medium that predated film – in this case, photography. At the same time, it reveals the behind-the-scenes workings of filmic technique, at once inviting viewers to conspire with the film, and alienating them from the fictional world it creates. In *Le Portrait spirite*, a man enters and holds up two signs side by side, one in French and one in English: 'Photographie spirite Effet fondu obtenu sans fond noir grande Nouveauté' and 'Spiritualistic photo Dissolving effect obtained without black background GREAT NOVELTY'. He exits, and Méliès runs in from the left, bows, and reaches out of view for a large wooden frame, over which he stretches a large sheet of white canvas, before inserting the structure into a larger gilt frame. He then ushers in a woman wearing a little sailor suit, wide-brimmed hat, black thigh-length stockings and white pumps; she bows to the audience. Méliès places a small footstool below the picture frame, which the woman uses to climb onto the platform on which the frame is standing; he then places the footstool on the platform, and she stands on it in front of the frame. Méliès circles his hand around his face, indicates the shape of the woman's body, and then gestures as if to present something to the audience. Reaching behind the frame, he takes a flame, which he sets down below the picture frame. He points back and forth between the fire and the woman, and as he undulates his arms, coaxing magic, the woman is transformed first into a sketch, and then into a more complete drawing of her likeness. Méliès removes the canvas from the gilt frame and, handling it like a bullfighter's cape, waves it to reveal the woman standing on top of the platform. She moves over to one end of the platform and bends over with her arms jutting out in front of her as if she were about to dive into water; Méliès takes a couple of articles of clothing from off camera and throws them at the woman. The clothes, a prim blouse and long skirt, appear to slip right onto her body. She and Méliès take a bow.

The bilingual signs at the beginning of this film announcing the use of a new special effect foreclose any suspension of disbelief, signalling the film's status as a cinematic spectacle. The message may be read not only in two languages, but also in two ways, to refer to the photographic process depicted in the diegesis, and to the non-diegetic film-making process. Although the film shows the magician transforming the woman into a representation of her, the notice at the beginning reveals that the agent of this transformation is actually the filmmaker.

Film's depiction as a form of latter-day magic is analogous to photography's status as a latter-day form of painting. In using a picture frame to display a photographic trick, Méliès is highlighting the transition between two representational modes – and eras. Similarly, magic functions both as an aid and a metaphor for filmic effects: the addition of the fire reinforces the aura of hocus pocus even as it distracts the eye from the dissolve being effected above it. The two transformational modes are merged in the opening notice, which links technology and magic in the phrase *photographie spirite* (and whose bilingual repetition points to another form of transformation, translation). The backdrop of the stone building shown opening out onto the forest – a man-made structure in the midst of nature – provides a visual analogy of the relationship between the picture of the woman and the woman herself. When the filmmaker takes the canvas out of its frame and uses it as a magician's cape (or sheet, as in *Escamotage d'une dame chez Robert-Houdin*) with which to bring the flesh-and-blood woman back to life, the cycle of mimetic representation is complete. Finally, when the blouse and skirt are thrown onto the woman at the end of the film, this ordinary outfit appears as the most artificial of costumes, because we have grown accustomed, even in the very short space of this film, to seeing the woman dressed as an overgrown doll (or space cadette, as in *Le Voyage dans la lune/A Trip to the Moon* (1902)). The film thus succeeds in emphasizing the artifice inherent in that which seems perfectly natural.

Le Roi du maquillage/Untamable Whiskers (1904), too, foregrounds the conventional nature of signification, by displaying a catalogue of different representational modes, each more arbitrarily motivated than the last. The film begins when Méliès enters with (unusually) a cigarette in his mouth, doffs his top hat, and bows to the camera. Behind him a backdrop depicts a bridge stretching over a river in front of a medieval city. He reaches off camera and pulls a blackboard into frame, on which he draws the head of a man with fringe, or bangs, and shoulder-length hair (in a style reminiscent of the prince in *Le Royaume des fées*). He points to the image, then points to his own face. He pushes away the blackboard, throws off his hat, and, facing the camera, holds out his hands in a gesture that is at once triumphant and expectant. Méliès stands closer to the camera than he ordinarily does, resulting in a medium (waist-up) shot, rather than the customary long (full-body) shot. As he stands still, a wig slowly dissolves onto his head resembling that of the chalk drawing. He smiles and gestures to the camera as if to say, 'You think that's good? Wait'll you see the next one!' He pulls the blackboard back into frame and draws another face: this one with a long moustache and craggy beard. He pushes the board off , and stands expectantly as he is slowly transformed through a dissolve into a man resembling the drawing (who also happens to resemble Rip Van Winkle from Méliès's film of 1905). This process is repeated with Méliès in mutton-chop whiskers and monocle; but then, instead of drawing another illustration on the chalkboard, he merely writes the English words, 'Comic excentric' (sic) before turning into a clown with a painted face. For his next transformation, he forgoes the chalkboard altogether and simply turns into a man with a Napoleon hat and moustache, before turning into Mephistopheles, throwing a cape over his shoulders and, finally, disappearing altogether.

This film is Méliès's most explicit engagement with intertextuality. The disguises he dons are recognizable as characters in other films of his: the prince, Mephistopheles – and Rip Van Winkle, a year before he actually made the film of the same name. (This film could be considered a distant precursor of television shows that occasionally show a 'memories' episode composed almost entirely of clips from earlier episodes.) By starting out in street clothes before turning into each of these characters, Méliès deconstructs the suspension of disbelief necessary for the creation of filmic illusion; moreover, the word 'maquillage', or makeup, in the title chips away at the realist aesthetic from the very beginning (the title would not have appeared on the film itself, but it would probably have been made known to viewers by the film's exhibitors). He is also recreating the film-making process, by first making sketches of the characters he will play and the costumes he will wear, before 'realising' them, or making them come to life.

In the course of this short film, we witness a progression from iconic representation based on resemblance (Méliès acquires the features of the face he has drawn) to symbolic representation based on an arbitrary link between the written word and its referent, which has been forged by convention rather than any inherent relation between sign and referent. What at first appears to be missing in this Peircean system is the indexical sign based on causality, but the illustrations on the chalkboard, as well as the words 'comic excentric', can be seen as indexical because they are depicted as the source of Méliès's transformations.[2] Unlike other films in which a drawing, painting, or sculpture itself comes to life, Pygmalion-like, this film presents drawing (or writing) as a prompt that has the magical power to transform the artist in its image (or in the image of its referent, as in the case of the words). Once again (as in *Le Portrait mystérieux*), the creator becomes the created. Representation here becomes decreasingly motivated by resemblance, resulting first in the disappearance of the sign (Méliès turns into the admiral and then into Mephistopheles without the aid of an illustrated or written prompt), and, finally, in the disappearance of the referent, as Méliès himself vanishes. The ultimate and logical extension of this progression is the disappearance of the entire semiotic universe: the film comes to an end.

Like *Le Roi du maquillage*, *Les Cartes vivantes/The Living Playing Cards* (1904) also relies on a logic of progression from one mode of representation to another. In this film, Méliès bows and points to an ornate bench at centre stage, which he taps with his stick and stomps on in order to demonstrate its solidity. He pulls a card from a deck lying on a small table and shows it to an assumed audience, approaching the camera, 'reacting' to the audience's presumed inability to see the card. Still reacting to the audience's supposed frustration, Méliès magically makes the normal-sized playing card larger-than-life in two stages, in a sleight-of-hand trick. He throws the card toward a large white board behind him, and the card disappears while the board is suddenly transformed into a giant nine of spades. Méliès then selects another playing card from the pack, rips it up, and sets it on fire beneath the giant nine of spades, which is transformed, in the famous dissolve on a white background, into the queen of hearts, with 'Judith' written on the upper right corner.

Méliès next climbs up to the giant card, points to the queen, and indicates a small set of stairs, which he then swishes down daintily, arms fluttering out to his sides in a camp rendition of a *femme fatale* (recalling his flamenco pose in *La Statue animée*). The

2 See Liszka 1996: 37–40.

illustrated queen dissolves to a real woman, whom he helps down the steps. Méliès lets the audience admire the living queen for a moment, kneels to kiss her hand, then assists her back up the steps, where she dissolves back into an illustration. Méliès selects another card, makes more gestures, this time indicating a long beard and moustache, and the illustrated queen dissolves to an illustrated king, Alexandre. As the magician bows triumphantly, a live king bursts through the white board from behind; feigning astonishment, Méliès runs off to the right as the corpulent king laughs heartily at the left of frame. The card itself is now blank with a single club in the upper left corner. The king suddenly throws off his costume, and we see that it is Méliès underneath. Méliès bows, turns his back to the camera, and runs toward the card, jumping toward it and disappearing, only to reappear peeking out from behind it. He climbs down and exits right, waving to the camera.

By approaching the camera with the nine of spades in his hand, Méliès manages to play on the limitations of both the theatre – with the audience a fixed distance from the stage – and early cinema, with the camera a fixed distance from its subject – at the same time. This prototype of a close-up recalls the reverse travelling shot used two years earlier in *L'Homme a la tête en caoutchouc/The Man with the Rubber Head* (1901). *Les Cartes vivantes*, in which an illustration turns into a real person, is a structural reversal of *Le Portrait spirite*, in which a real woman turns into a drawing.

This film signals the transition from stage illusion to filmic illusion made possible by editing: at first, the conjuror relies on theatrical sleight-of-hand to make the cards grow bigger, but then switches to substitution splicing. When Méliès takes the place of Alexandre at the end of the film, he is suggesting that he is the king of the cinema, the modern-day equivalent of a monarch, whose power extends as far as his image is displayed. Méliès would repeat the trick of bursting through a screen in 1929 at the gala held in his honour at the Salle Pleyel, when he made his grand entrance by walking through the large screen on which several of his films had been projected.

As we saw in *Le Portrait mystérieux*, the representation here merges with the representer when the animated Alexandre becomes

Méliès, the magician who has brought him(self) to life. Even when these representations appear to take on a life of their own, to exceed themselves and their creator, they turn out to be entirely in the magician's control – even characters as powerful as Alexander the Great, who conquered much of the globe, and Judith, mighty heroine who saved a whole city by committing an act of murder – even these formidable personalities are contained by and in Méliès himself, who brings them to life or turns them back into illustrations as he pleases.

As in *Les Cartes vivantes*, drawings come to life in *Les Affiches en goguette/The Hilarious Posters* (1906); but whereas in the previous film a magician called the shots, here characters take on a life of their own. A backdrop containing seven posters surrounding a larger rectangular space with the words *cadre réservé* fills the screen. The posters contain advertisements for phoney products, including 'Le Tripolin', modelled on the enamel paint known as *ripolin* (a brand name that has become a common designation for enamel paint). A worker enters and sticks up a poster in the empty space advertising a show at the Parisiana music hall, *L'Amour à crédit* (Love on the Installment Plan). The worker exits and two policemen stroll by. When they are out of frame, the illustrations suddenly come to life: actors perch on tiny square stages built on top of each other. The cavorting couple in the Parisiana ad jump out of their frame and chat with characters from the other ads, sampling their wares; when the man becomes overly friendly with the woman promoting corsets, his partner kicks him. The Tripolin poster now comes to life in a superimposed shot of three men bent over to resemble the illustrated ad; they laugh uproariously and dance around manically, considerably smaller than the other characters, who begin to throw things at each other. The posters become illustrations again as a couple of unsuspecting policemen stroll past from left to right. A distinguished-looking man wanders in; as he pauses in front of the Parisiana poster, all the posters come to life again, but this time, with the three Tripolin men squeezed into their square without the aid of superimposition. The characters all throw various objects at the passer-by; four policemen enter and general mayhem ensues, with feathers and flour flying everywhere. The policemen attempt to push the characters back inside, and the posters become inanimate once more. As the cops congratulate themselves, the entire flat collapses on top of them, tearing over their heads to reveal the human characters laughing and waving from behind a tall iron gate. The cops attempt to climb on the gate, but one of them gets caught on it, dangling by the seat of his pants. The flat stands again to reveal a policeman-sized tear in the Tripolin square. The cast of human characters dances gleefully past the helpless policemen, left poking through the flat.

Méliès seems to have gone to great lengths to set off the Tripolin poster from the rest of the advertisements. First, it is the only square left blank when the posters come to life for the first time. We are thus inclined to pay special attention to its contents when they are filled in, although this is not difficult, because when the square does 'come to life' it is apparent that it is the only one whose characters have been superimposed, making them smaller and more mobile than the characters in the other squares. Then, it is the square that the policemen's heads poke through when the flat falls, leaving a hole in it. The fact that this space is used to advertise a brand of paint, and shows men painting a wall, thematizes pictoral representation. The spoof name for the paint, Tripolin, in addition to naming the number of men in the advertisement (tri/three), plays on the word *tripot*, or seedy dive, and *tripotage*, or shady dealings, where deception is the name of the game. The alternation between the painted posters and the live characters is comparable to the alternation between the theatrical device of the stage boxes and the filmic effect of superimposition in the Tripolin box.

This short film shows advertising running rampant, commercialism run amok – even love, in the Parisiana poster, is offered *à crédit*. The fact that Méliès was the first in Europe, and the second in the world, to make filmed advertisements (in 1898), combined with his struggle to remain independent from bigger production companies, made him well aware of the immense power of commercial interests. In addition to a handful of advertising films, Méliès also engaged in product placement in some of his films: in the 1901 *Barbe-bleue*, an enormous bottle of champagne, the brand-name of Mercier clearly visible, is paraded past as kitchen staff prepare the wedding banquet; and in *Le Tunnel sous la Manche/Tunnelling the English Channel* (1906), workers on the French side indulge in some Vin du Loupillon (though this is more of a joke at the expense of the President of the Republic, who had a financial interest in this particular vineyard, than an actual advertisement). Most of all, though, Méliès advertised his own products – the Théâtre Robert-Houdin (as we saw in *Le Portrait mystérieux*), and his Star-Film company, in many of his films. In the 1897 *Entre Calais et Douvres/Between Calais and Dover*, he promotes both of his home-grown ventures in a sign on the ship that bears the name 'Robert-Houdin Star Line'; and in *Le Palais des Mille et une nuits/The Palace of the Arabian Nights* (1905), a sign built obtrusively into the scenery, over which characters must walk in order to make their entrances and exits, reads, 'Copyrighted by Geo Méliès 1905 Paris New York'.

Les Affiches en goguette shows representations going out of control, getting the better of the forces that would contain them (here, appropriately, police officers). If representations are only 'pretending' to be representations, if they are 'really' real, then, conversely, it is equally possible that real people and things are actually representations pretending to be real. By erasing the bar between signifier and signified, the characters in the ads risk ending up behind bars: it is up to the meaning police to replace and reinforce the barrier between signifier and signified, but their efforts backfire. When the set collapses to reveal an outdoor setting, we see reality exceeding representation (an effect that Méliès achieves by yielding to a more realistic mode of representation).

In fact, this trend toward realism is what is often cited as the cause of Méliès's downfall, as his fanciful films were being passed over increasingly for more realistic films. Partly in response to this trend, Méliès did try his hand at several overtly realist films around this time; *Les Affiches en goguette* may thus be read as an autobiographical comment on the difficulties in doing so. In *La Providence de Notre-Dame-des-Flots/The Providence of the Waves, or the Dream of a Poor Fisherman* (1904), an impoverished fisherman's family is rescued by passers-by. In *Détresse et Charité/ The Christmas Angel*, made the same year, an indigent young beggar girl collapses in the snow: in the Anglo-American version, she is saved by a couple of passing automobilists who take her home and shower her family with gifts; in the version made for French audiences, the child freezes to death and her soul is carried to heaven by the Christmas angel (Malthête 1996: 117) (these differences suggest that the American audience's predilection for a happy ending was already well in place by the turn of the century). In 1906, Méliès made *Les Incendiaires*, alternatively titled *L'Histoire d'un crime/A Desperate Crime*, a story about a bandit who sets fire to a farm and is arrested and beheaded. Frazer notes that '[t]his final scene had to be suppressed because it was too graphic and realistic' (1979: 169).

These films were not Méliès's only foray into realist filmmaking, however. In the course of his career, he made two other types of realist film: newsreel footage devoid of tricks and supernatural situations, and *actualités reconstituées*. But even these more conventionally realistic films, like those that explicitly thematize representation, show the considerable artifice involved in creating the illusion of realism.

Documentary footage and *actualités reconstituées*

Though Méliès is not commonly associated with documentary or newsreel footage, Jacques Malthête counts ninety-three films *pris-sur-le-vif* (made on location), or 18% of Méliès's total production (Malthête 1995: 72). The vast majority of these films have disappeared, but a copy of *Panorama pris d'un train en marche/Panorama from the Top of a Moving Train* (1898) can be found at the NFA. In this brief film, less than a minute long, the camera, pointed straight ahead, is attached to the front of a train that appears to be travelling at normal speed. The train approaches a tunnel, then travels through it and out the other side; it approaches and travels through two more tunnels. Each time the train goes through a tunnel, the light at the other end resembles a large eye that opens wider as the train approaches it. A stream of smoke rises from the train's smokestack and invades the screen. The film ends abruptly.

This film, more than any other extant film made by Méliès, would seem to be a slice of life, unadorned by staging, elaborate scenery and costumes, or complicated editing effects. At first glance, it seems to offer nothing more than the sensation of speed gained by glimpsing a bit of the world from atop a moving train – a sensation that is no longer sensational, having lost its ability to enthrall today's audiences, but which, at the time of the film's production, was undoubtedly thrilling. But even this straight-forward piece of footage manages to be self-referential: the giant opening eye at the end of each tunnel suggests that, above all, this film is about seeing, and about the camera's capacity to provide an eye looking out onto the world. Not only is this one of the first travelling shots in the history of cinema, it is also an early point-of-view shot, as the camera assumes the perspective of the train.[3] Finally, no film made by Méliès would be complete without a bit of magic: here, the train literally disappears in a puff of smoke.

Méliès also made a number of recreations of current events, including natural disasters, accidents, wars, ceremonial state occasions, and the Dreyfus Affair. Rather than going to the site of these newsworthy events, however, Méliès recreated them in his studio, inventing a genre called *actualités reconstituées*, an oxymoron combining contemporaneity and retrospection, which might best be translated as 'old news'.[4] Before the advent of the newsreel (the first *journal d'actualités filmées*, or newsreel, was created by Pathé in 1908: Pathé-fait-divers),[5] these films provided news-hungry audiences with life-like depictions of events that they would otherwise only read about in the newspapers. Méliès went to great lengths to base his sets and costumes on descriptions and drawings that appeared in the illustrated press (such as *L'Illustration* and *Le Petit Journal*). In 1961, René Jeanne and Charles Ford dismissed

3 The first travelling shot was created by Promio, one of Lumière's cameramen, who in 1896 attached a camera to a gondola in Venice (Frazer 1979: 66).

4 The first film of this genre, *l'Explosion du Cuirassé Maine*, was made by Méliès in 1898; others include *La Guerre gréco-turque* (1899), and *Les Incendiaires* (1902).

5 See Huret 1984: 28.

what they called 'les actualités postiches' ('phoney newsreels') as 'cet amusant petit jeu que l'on peut regarder comme un véritable abus de confiance puisqu'il visait – et réussissait – à tromper nombre de ceux qui en étaient les spectateurs' (Jeanne & Ford 1961: 6).[6] This assessment, however, does not take into account the attitudes and expectations of contemporary viewers, who were perfectly accustomed to seeing drawings of current events in the newspapers. Yet, for all their topicality and attention to realist detail, these films, too, acknowledged the realist illusion. I will examine the extant *actualités reconstituées* in chronological order, with the exception of *L'Affaire Dreyfus*, Méliès's most important *actualité*, which I will discuss at greater length at the end of this chapter.

Combat naval en Grèce/Naval Combat in Greece (1897) is not discussed in either Frazer or Hammond; presumably, this is because it was not known to be extant, or was not available for viewing until more recently. The film depicts a scene from the Greco-Turkish War. We see a ship's deck from head on. The arrangement of the set is very similar to that of *Entre Calais et Douvres/Between Calais and Dover*, a fiction film made the same year, but here the ship is clearly a battleship. Sailors – unusually, for Méliès, played by men – appear at a door upstage and climb up onto the deck, toward the camera. A captain with a telescope supervises the sailors, who make their way to a cannon at the left of the frame. The captain then turns to face downstage, looking through his telescope directly at the camera; the sailors, too, look in the direction of the camera. There are two explosions of smoke, which gradually clears, revealing one sailor lying on the deck. The others throw water on him.

The captain's direct glance at the camera challenges the implicit barrier between viewers and viewed. This challenge is reinforced by the fact that he holds a telescope up to the film-viewing audience, the better to see us with. This is different from the playing to the camera that Tom Gunning (Elsaesser 1990: 57) identifies as a key feature of the cinema of attractions, because Méliès here transforms the film audience into a character with an

6 'that amusing little game that may be regarded as a veritable breach of trust because it succeeded in fooling many of those who watched it'.

active role in the film, thus presenting the scene from the point of view of a diegetically present but physically absent character: we return the favour by blasting a cannonball onto the ship.

The following year, Méliès made *Visite sous-marine du Maine/ Divers at Work on the Wreck of the Maine* (1898). This is the final and only known surviving episode of a five-part series that depicts Spain's bombing of the US battleship Maine in the port of Havana, triggering the Spanish-American War. The other episodes were *Collision et Naufrage en Mer, Quais de la Havane, Explosion du Cuirassé 'Le Maine'*, and *Visite de l'Epave du 'Maine'* (Malthête 1981: 56). In this extant episode, two men in diving gear attached to long hoses search through the wreckage of a sunken ship at the bottom of the sea; one of the men climbs into a hole in the ship, disappearing out of view. A third diver descends a rope ladder into frame and the other man emerges from the hole in the ship carrying a corpse (a floppy dummy in a white sailor suit), which is tied to a dangling hose and hoisted out of frame. One of the divers brings a trunk from the ship's interior, sets it down, and climbs the rope ladder. The film ends here – and not a moment too soon, because the dangling hoses were starting to become entangled.

This film exhibits the circular structure that Marshall Deutelbaum identified in many Lumière films, and which, for him, suggests the presence of a coherent, if skeletal, narrative (Deutelbaum 1979). If Lumière's *Sortie d'usine* (1895) begins with the opening of a door and ends with a door closing, in Méliès's film, a diver enters the ship and ultimately re-emerges, while one diver climbs down the rope ladder into frame, and another climbs up the same ladder and out of frame moments later. Méliès combined these narrative techniques with an attention to realist detail that heightened the film's sense of illusion. For example, he placed a gauze screen in front of the camera, which gave the scene an undulating, watery feel. This was also the first time that he shot through a fish tank, complete with live fish, an effect that would be repeated in *Le Voyage dans la lune, Le Royaume des fées*, and *La Sirène/The Mermaid* (1904). The real fish swimming about in the frame add a metonymic veneer of realism to the scene. The presence of the dummy representing a dead sailor creates a similarly realistic effect, but by very different means: it is by virtue of their *contrast* with the obviously fake sailor that the other aspects of the scene are made to seem all the more authentic.

Similarly, *Le Sacre d'Edouard VII/The Coronation of King Edward VII* (1902) also combines artifice with a display of realism that ultimately invites viewers to question the distinction between the two representational modes. After *L'Affaire Dreyfus*, this film is the most celebrated of Méliès's *actualités reconstituées*. *Sacre d'Édouard VII* is actually a 'pre-enactment', having been made before the coronation, which was postponed from 26 June to 9 August because of Edward's ill health. The film premiered in London on the evening of the actual coronation, sandwiched between footage of the royal coach arriving and leaving Westminster (Hammond 1974: 53–4). The proximity of the newsreel footage to the re-enactment confers a metonymic effect of realism on the latter, much like the placement of live fish in front of the artificial set in *Visite sous-marine du Maine*. The film is not numbered in Méliès's catalogue, because it was commissioned by Charles Urban, managing director of the Warwick Trading Company, who would go on to manage Méliès's London office. According to Jacques Malthête, Méliès filmed two versions of the *Sacre*, one for Urban and the other for Biograph in Washington. It was shortly after making this film that Méliès began filming with two cameras simultaneously, sending one of the negatives to New York for immediate copyright (Malthête 1989: 9–11).

Urban supplied Méliès with much advance information about the protocol of the ceremony, and many directives concerning the film's production. In a letter to Méliès, dated 5 June 1902, he writes: 'If necessary get the services of accomplished actors to take the part of the King and Queen. The make-ups [sic] or imperson-ations must be perfect. In reality the King is several inches shorter than the Queen, but this must not show in the picture. The King is very sensitive on this point, and always wishes to appear slightly taller than the Queen.'[7] The 'accomplished actors' who ended up playing the roles of the king and queen were actually a wash-house

7 Fonds Méliès, Collection Cinémathèque Française, Bibliothèque du Film (MÉLIÈS 1).

attendant, the same actor who would reprise the role of the English monarch in *Le Tunnel sous la Manche*, and a dancer from the Châtelet troupe. King Edward himself, upon viewing Méliès's film, is said to have commented (although probably not in French):

> Si je ne savais que le roi et la reine du film ne sont que des sosies, je serais persuadé que nous nous voyions en personne tant la ressemblance est parfaite! ... Toutes mes félicitations! C'est splendide! Mais quel merveilleux appareil que le cinéma. Il a trouvé le moyen d'enregistrer même les parties de la cérémonie qui n'ont pas eu lieu. Ça, c'est réellement fantastique![8]

Frazer (1979: 100) notes that the film depicts rites that were ultimately eliminated in the actual ceremony to avoid overtaxing the king. Yet Edward himself, in deeming the film to be 'réellement fantastique', characterized it more accurately than he may have realised. Although Méliès took great pains to recreate the ceremony held in Westminster Abbey down to the last detail, there is evidence to suggest that he had to be dissuaded from injecting the film with an overtly fantastical element. As Urban warned in a letter dated 26 May 1902, 'Another suggestion which it is advisable not to carry out, is to have the vision of Queen Victoria appear. This would not be pleasing to the better class people [sic] although I have no doubt it would do well with the cheap [showmen]'.[9] Although Méliès ultimately suppressed the impulse to turn the coronation into *Phantom of the Opera*, his film nonetheless contains many theatrical elements.

It is perhaps no accident that for the most ambitious of his 'realist' films, Méliès chose to depict an elaborately staged ceremony, characterized by its performative function ('performative' in both the theatrical and linguistic senses of the word: the ceremonial gestures have a highly choreographed quality, and their performance not only represents a transformation of Edward's civil status,

---

8 'If I didn't know that the king and queen in the film were impersonators, I'd be convinced that we were looking at ourselves, so perfect is the resemblance! ... Many congratulations! This is splendid! What a marvellous apparatus cinema is. It's found a way of recording even the parts of the ceremony that didn't take place. Now that's really fantastic!' Cited in Jeanne and Ford 1961: 182.

9 The last word is difficult to read, and might be something else.

but actually brings it about, like a wedding ceremony). In many ways, Méliès's staging of the coronation resembles one of his *féeries* or magic acts. When the attendants point and bow to the camera while making carefully pantomined gestures, they could just as well be the pointy-hatted scientists making their entrance at the beginning of *Voyage dans la lune* or, for that matter, Méliès the magician bowing and gesturing impresario-like before performing a magic trick. Later, two of the bewigged attendants dressed in knee breeches and tights (like many of the courtiers in Méliès's fairytales) remove Edward's cloak in much the same way that assistants would remove a magician's cape. When, finally, at the end of the film, all of the actors except the king and queen appear to be waving to the camera, they may be imitating an actual part of the coronation ceremony, but the effect is not unlike the curtain call with which many of Méliès's earlier films based on magic acts conclude.

The interplay between fantasy and realism manifested in *Le Sacre d'Edouard VII* was the logical outcome of a tradition that had begun early in Méliès's career. The stage had been set for *Edouard* in 1899, by Méliès's most elaborate and controversial *actualité*, *L'Affaire Dreyfus*.

Framing Dreyfus

In 1899, Méliès made a series of eleven one-minute non-fiction films about the Dreyfus Affair as it was still unfolding, portraying sympathetically Dreyfus's arrest, his imprisonment on Devil's Island and his return to France for a retrial. *L'Affaire Dreyfus/The Dreyfus Affair* has sometimes been referred to as Méliès's longest film at the time it was made, but two modern sources assert that the films were made to be sold separately,[10] and Méliès himself wrote that 'La première vue qui dépassa la longueur courante (17 mètres) fut une *Cendrillon*', which was made immediately after *L'Affaire Dreyfus* (Malthête-Méliès 1982: 23).[11]

10 See Malthête *et al.* 1981: 70, and Malthête-Méliès 1982.
11 'The first film that exceeded the then-common length of 17 metres was one of the Cinderella films.'

The series provoked partisan fistfights, which led to its censorship in France, and to the censorship of all other films on the subject until 1950.[12] Georges Sadoul called *L'Affaire Dreyfus* 'le premier film "engagé"' ('the first politically engaged film') (1970: 28); apart from his brief stint as an anti-Boulangist satirical cartoonist for his cousin's review *La Griffe* ten years earlier, this is Méliès's only known expression of political commitment. Because the film portrayed Dreyfus sympathetically at a time when everyone had a passionate opinion about the Affair, it could therefore be considered to be pro-Dreyfus. For today's viewers, it is not always easy to discern the sympathetic elements of the films, but the abundance of huffy gesturing and self-righteous facial expressions on the part of Dreyfus make of him a dignified hero who refuses to be degraded by the accusations made against him. (The enormous crucifix in the courtroom, shown in the upper centre of the frame in Méliès's film, is, in a more literal sense perhaps than Barthes (1994: 26–7) intended, a *punctum*, the detail that wounds, the stigma evoking at once Dreyfus's similarity to the Christian icon through a shared martydom, and his alienation from Christianity, through his Jewish heritage.)

Méliès's series, however, dramatized much more than the Affair itself. It also dramatized the transition between two modes of documentary representation, the written and the filmic. Méliès's career ran parallel to that of the nineteenth-century litterateur to whom the new mass media gave a voice in politics. According to Susan Buck-Morss, the new mass readership engendered by the appearance of the *feuilleton*, or serialized novel, in newspapers drew authors into national politics: 'One has only to regard the format of a nineteenth-century newspaper, in which the *feuilleton* occupied the bottom quarter of the front page, to see, literally, how thin was the line between political fact and literary fiction. News stories were literary constructions; feuilleton novelists used news stories as content. The tendency of mass media is to render the distinction between art and politics meaningless' (Buck-Morss 1989: 140). It is no accident that the birth of the intellectual

12 For an account of the controversy the film evoked, see Malthête-Méliès 1995: 220.

coincided with the birth of the filmmaker, with the birth of film – that specifically French variety of intellectual, who has an influential opinion on important events of the day, is indeed a product of the mass media. The mass diffusion of 'expert' opinions in print was quickly complemented by the use of film as a medium of political expression. While the written discourse of intellectuals in France remains uniquely influential to this day, the mass diffusion of political discourse throughout the twentieth century would increasingly come to take place through visual media.

Throughout *L'Affaire Dreyfus*, the prominence accorded to written documents is striking; in almost every tableau or episode, the action almost invariably centres upon a character who is reading or writing, thus calling attention to both the similarities and the differences between filmic and written documents.

To a certain extent, the central role of writing in Méliès's film series can be attributed to the importance of written documents in the Dreyfus Affair itself. The charge of espionage against Captain Alfred Dreyfus, a French army officer from a Jewish French-Alsatian family, hinged on a number of written documents: first, there was the anonymously authored *bordereau*, or note containing state secrets that was discovered in the German military attaché's office. Then, there were the samples of Dreyfus's handwriting said to resemble the writing on the *bordereau*, including the note containing the words of the *bordereau* that the commander du Paty de Clam dictated to Dreyfus, and which led to the latter's arrest. There was also the secret dossier shown to the judges in closed chambers but not to the defence, which contained vague allusions to 'ce canaille de D' ('that scoundrel, D'). And, in 1896, there was a letter mentioning Dreyfus that appeared to have been written by the Italian military attaché to his German counterpart. This document, which turned out to have been fabricated by the colonel Henry, would come to be known as 'le faux Henry'. In addition to these documents, there were any number of texts that, while not central to the case itself, played an important role in the Affair – what Gérard Genette would call paratexts (Genette 1987: 7), such as the flurry of newspaper articles and pamphlets written sometimes to inform but more often to persuade, of which Zola's

'J'accuse' remains the best-known, and many of which were read by Méliès before and during production of his film series.

Considering the importance of documents in the Affair itself, it is not surprising that writing and reading feature prominently in Méliès's filmed account.[13] The series opens with Du Paty de Clam dictating the contents of the *bordereau* to Dreyfus, who copies them down. In the next available episode, Dreyfus is shown on Devil's Island first reading a book, and then reading a letter delivered to him by a soldier. In the third instalment, two soldiers read aloud from a piece of paper ordering them to shackle a now prematurely aged Dreyfus to his bed. In the next instalment, colonel Henry sits at a desk writing a letter, which he seals in an envelope before slitting his throat. It ends with soldiers opening Henry's letter upon discovering his body. In the fifth episode, notable for its innovative rain and lightning effects, Dreyfus is shown disembarking in Brittany upon his return from the Ile du Diable for the second trial. Before he is led off the boat, another man emerges who hands a letter and a sheaf of papers to an officer waiting on the dock, and the two discuss the papers.[14] The sixth instalment opens with Dreyfus writing yet again, while sitting at a desk in his cell in Rennes. He then walks across the room and picks up a booklet, which he looks through before showing it to his lawyers, who have since entered the cell. In the next instalment, which depicts the attack on Dreyfus's lawyer, maître Labori (played by Méliès), Labori is shown intently discussing a sheaf of papers with the colonal Picquart and the mayor of Rennes before being shot. The scene ends when, the mayor and Picquart

---

13 I refer to the copy at the National Film Archive of the British Film Institute, which, at nine episodes/739 feet, is the most complete copy available anywhere. This copy is missing the second episode, which depicts Dreyfus's military degradation, and the final episode, which shows people leaving the building where the second trial was held.

14 This episode is notable for the movement of characters (along the camera axis), as the group of soldiers, shown from behind, lead Dreyfus away from the camera. This deep staging has not before, to my knowledge, been pointed out in regard to this scene, but it has been discussed in relation to two other scenes, the *Attentat contre maître Labori* and the *Bagarre entre journalistes*. See Brewster, 'Deep Staging in French Films 1900–1914,' in Elsaesser 1990: 45–55, and Jenn 1984: 20 and 24.

having run off in pursuit of the attacker, Labori's cries for help are ignored by passers-by until a man comes along (reading something written on a piece of paper) who stops and helps. Although the eighth episode, referred to as *La Bagarre entre journalistes*, which is cited along with the *Attentat contre maître Labori* as an early example of deep staging, is notable for its absence of images of writing, writing is certainly implicit in the fact that the whole scene revolves around journalists. The final episode available shows Dreyfus and his lawyers arguing his case at the Lycée de Rennes, site of his second trial. Here, too, although writing is not depicted explicitly, its presence in the law is implicit. (I'll come back to these two episodes that don't actually show writing or reading taking place, in order to discuss what might be replacing them.)

Méliès's serial film could thus be said to make a spectacle of writing, as it documents the function of documents. The film both depicts journalists (as in the famous 'bagarre' scene) and is modelled on journalistic accounts and illustrations (Méliès freely copied images and descriptions from *Le Petit Journal illustré* and *l'Illustration* for his sets, staging, and costumes, down to the most minute detail). This nostalgia for writing was reflected in film generally, which retained the ghostly presence of writing as an afterimage. The first newsreels, created in 1908, were given names like the *Pathé-Journal* and the *Eclair-journal* (Deslandes 1963: 66), names that evoked film's writerly origins, as did the term for the Lumières' invention, the *cinématographe*, literally writer of motion, and later expressions such as *caméra-stylo*, cinematic *écriture*, and the *auteur* theory of cinema.

The Dreyfus films' emphasis on the role of the document in the establishment of truth, coupled with the films' implicit claim to be a representation of the truth, established film's potential to be a new form of document, in both senses of the word, depending on the context (that is, as a narrative or non-narrative account granted historical validity retrospectively, or as a certificate of authenticity; in the case of the latter, the document would stand up in court as legal testimony; in the case of the former, which would include *actualités reconstituées*, the document would serve as a witness to history). Today, Méliès's serial films would be classed under the heading 'non-fiction film', 'docu-drama', or, if televised, 'reality programming'. The films' status as a re-enactment mirrored – or re-enacted – their subject, because re-enactment played a central role in the Affair itself.

The first episode of Méliès's film begins with Dreyfus being made to re-enact the writing of the *bordereau*, which leads to his arrest. Dreyfus's second trial was something of a re-enactment of the first: both were conducted in extremely irregular conditions, and both concluded with an erroneous verdict of guilt. Similarly, the trial of Émile Zola, famous for his promotion and practice of a realist literary aesthetic that purported to hold a mirror up to everyday life, could be seen as a re-enactment of the first Dreyfus trial. Even the personal mail sent to the prisoner on the Ile du Diable was copied over, according to Pierre Vidal-Naquet in his preface to Dreyfus's personal account of the affair: 'Il reçoit parfois, pas toujours, des livres, des revues du courrier, mais ce courrier, à partir de mars 1897, est un courrier recopié. Les autorités vivent dans la terreur d'un système cryptographique' (Dreyfus 1994: 6).[15] Finally, the forged document that Henry produced in order to cover up the lack of evidence against Dreyfus completes the cycle of reproduction inherent in the Affair even before Méliès came along to reproduce newspaper images and accounts of it in his film.

Re-enactment is antithetical to the aesthetics of aura, which Walter Benjamin describes, in 'The Work of Art in the Age of Mechanical Reproduction', in terms of a unique authenticity, precisely that which defies reproduction (Benjamin 1989: 217–51). It is also at the heart of the oft-cited dichotomy between Méliès and Lumière, or staged films and newsreel films made *sur le vif*. The very status of documents as proof, witness to events, evokes an aesthetic of the aura, or what Derrida would call a metaphysics of presence.[16] The newsreel, for example, subscribes to this aesthetic: you must go 'on location' to capture the unique, authentic

15 'He sometimes, but not always, received books and journals in the mail, but this mail was copied from March 1897. The authorities were paranoid that Dreyfus might be receiving encoded messages.'

16 For a discussion of the metaphysics of presence, see Derrida 1976: 12.

event. However, Méliès, in recreating the event, was rehearsing the function of mechanical reproduction itself. You don't need to go to the courtroom, he was implying; you can cobble together a set anywhere, anytime, with anyone, and still produce a (reproducible) image of the event. Méliès's re-enactment films, to the extent that they show us anything at all, are indexical, but what they indicate is theatrical: what they show us, in other words, is already a representation. In filming staged recreations of events, Méliès was displacing the function of documentaries, which dissipate the aura of a unique event by recording it and making it endlessly reproducible, both through repetition – the event may be viewed over and over – and through replication – any number of prints of the film may be made from the negative. In making filmed re-enactments, Méliès was shattering the illusion of a unique event before he even turned on the camera, thereby replacing the auratic at the pro-filmic level, instead of waiting to dissolve it at the moment of the mechanical reproduction of the event in its recording onto film. He was thus ahead of his time, a postmodernist *avant la lettre*.

The *Faux Dreyfus*, or the Doublier Affair

In 1898, Francis Doublier, a cameraman employed by the Lumière brothers, sought to capitalize on the widespread interest in the Dreyfus Affair by screening film extracts depicting shadowy images of French soldiers, a building, and a warship. Doublier's running commentary to accompany the film footage, a normal phenomenon before the introduction of intertitles around 1903, explained that one of the soldiers shown was Dreyfus, that the building spectators saw before them was the scene of his trial, and that the warship was carrying Dreyfus off to Devil's Island. During one of the showings of the film, a spectator stood up and, although he did not yell 'J'accuse', insisted that the film was not what it appeared. Doublier protested, but was finally forced to admit the film was a fake when the spectator reminded everyone that the first two scenes, which were reputed to show events that had occurred in 1894 and early 1895, would have predated the birth of cinema. The outrage caused by this duplicity (committed, incidentally, by a man whose very name suggests doubling) caused the film to be pulled from distribution (Sand 1994: 224).

This incident begs the question: why, if audiences objected to Doublier's film, did they not object to Méliès's re-enactment? Although some viewers objected to the subject-matter itself, as the series's history of censorship suggests, few had qualms about the films' representational status. Perhaps because in documentary terms, like the 'faux Henry', Méliès's film itself was a fake – only there was no cover-up, which is, after all, what sparked the Affair's most heated debates. It was this disingenuousness that Zola contrasted with outright fantasy in order to praise the latter: 'le charme de la féerie est pour moi dans la franchise de la convention, tandis que je suis, par contre, fâché de l'hypocrisie de cette convention, dans la comédie et le drame ... Et, d'ailleurs, une féerie n'est pas même un mensonge, elle est un conte auquel personne ne peut se tromper. Rien de bâtard en elle, elle est toute fantaisie. L'auteur y confesse qu'il entend rester dans l'impossible' (Zola 1968: 500).[17] If he was going to be lied to, Zola insisted on being told he was being lied to (apparently unconcerned by the resulting aporia). It was the pretence to reality, rather than to realism, that offended film audiences; or, more precisely, the claim of having been there, of co-presence, of eye-witness accountancy (or auratic authenticity). The difference between Méliès's film and Doublier's is the difference between reproduction and forgery, a difference that is in turn based on a metaphysics of presence: a reproduction is not presumed to have been present at the event it depicts, whereas a forgery is a text presumed to have been written by a certain person in a certain place at a certain moment – it claims to be the palpable relic of a particular act of writing or

17 'the charm of the fantasy play for me lies in its candid evocation of convention, whereas I am put off by the hypocritical use of this convention in comedy and drama ... What's more, there is nothing duplicitous about a fantasy play, which cannot be mistaken for anything other than a fable. There is nothing illegitimate about it; it is pure fantasy, in which the author admits the intention to remain in the realm of the impossible.'

recording. This metaphysics of presence also underlies the opposition between documentary film, with its 'you are there' or *pris sur le vif* aesthetic, and mise en scène, or what Méliès called 'scènes composées' – the traditional dichotomy, in other words, between Lumière and Méliès.[18]

For how can this dichotomy be maintained if the Affair itself already, in many ways, resembled a mise en scène? First, there were the costumes: Roger Shattuck writes that Dreyfus's uniform was 'visibly padded' – *doublé* – when he returned from Devil's Island for the second trial, so that he would not appear too pathetic and scrawny (Shattuck 1969: 16). Then, there were the comments in the press about the theatrical atmosphere of the proceedings: H. Bourgeois, in his 8 September 1899 column for *Le Petit journal* (2), wrote: 'En dépit des événements graves qui s'y déroulent, d'où sortiraient les destinées de la France, on ne peut s'empêcher de comparer l'auditoire à celui qui se presse au Moulin-Rouge, aux matinées du dimanche. C'est un scandale'.[19] The day before, Bourgeois had written: 'Un appareil cinématographique a été installé rue Toullier devant la porte de sortie du lycée et fonctionne au moment où l'on quitte le palais universitaire. Tout le monde voudrait être photographié, surtout les dames, qui s'avancent vers l'appareil en des poses qu'elles s'efforcent de rendre naturelles. C'est très amusant' (7 septembre 1899: 2).[20]

There was also the observation made by Zola, who mused, 'A-t-on remarqué que cette affaire, ce drame géant qui remue l'univers, semble mis en scène par quelque dramaturge sublime' (cited in Drouin 1994: 549).[21] Finally, Dreyfus's own account of

18 For a deconstruction of the dichotomy between Lumière and Méliès, see Gunning, '"Primitive" Cinema: A Frame-up? Or The Trick's on Us,' in Elsaesser 1990: 95–103.

19 'In spite of the serious events unfolding there, which would shape France's destinies, it is difficult not to compare the audience to the masses who crowd into the Moulin-Rouge for the Sunday matinées. It's a scandal.'

20 'A cinematographic device has been set up in front of the exit to the school on Toullier Street, and is turned on as people are leaving. Everyone wants to be photographed, especially the ladies, who approach the camera while trying to act natural. It's all very amusing.'

21 'Has anyone noticed that this affair, this huge, earth-shaking drama, seems to have been staged by some sublime playwright?'

his belated discovery of the furore caused by his case describes it as a 'narrative', a 'dramatic story': 'Puis M. Demange me fit succinctement le récit de l''Affaire'. J'écoutai haletant et dans mon esprit peu à peu s'enchaînèrent tous les anneaux de cette dramatique histoire' (Dreyfus 1994: 214).[22]

Like the border between reality and mise en scène in the Affair itself, the opposition between fantasy and realism within cinema has always been difficult to maintain. Georges Sadoul was one of the first to note that Méliès's fantastical tricks would eventually become the standard techniques of realist film-making: 'Mais ces formulettes magiques constitutaient, en réalité, les germes de la syntaxe, du langage, des moyens d'expression qui permirent au cinéma de traduire la réalité de la vie, mieux, sans doute, qu'aucun art avant lui' (Sadoul 1947: 26).[23] This point was reiterated by Edgar Morin in Le Cinéma ou l'homme imaginaire (1956: 59), and then again by Jean Mitry, who wrote: 'le réel n'est pas autre chose qu'un fantastique auquel nous sommes habitués' (Mitry 1990: 489);[24] Christian Metz then repeated the point in slightly more general terms in 1968: 'le trucage merveilleux peut à tout moment devenir convention dans le cinéma réaliste' (Metz 1968: 185).[25]

Méliès himself recognized the fantastical potential of the new medium upon viewing it for the first time, as he proclaimed it 'un truc extraordinaire' ('an extraordinary trick') (Malthête-Méliès 1973: 157). In a 1912 piece in L'Écho du Cinéma entitled 'Le Merveilleux au Cinéma', Méliès describes the nuts and bolts of technological development in terms that seem to undermine the medium's pretension to reproduce reality: 'chaque jour nous amène des inventions nouvelles, grâce au développement *fantastique* pris par

---

22 'Then Mr Demange briefly narrated the tale of the 'Affair'. I listened, breathless, as my mind gradually pieced together the various sections of this dramatic story.'

23 'But these magic spells constituted, in reality, the seeds of the syntax, language, and means of expression that enabled cinema to translate life's reality, probably better than any art before it.'

24 'The real is nothing other than a form of the fantastic to which we have become accustomed.'

25 'special effects can at any moment become conventional features of realist cinema'.

cette industrie' (Méliès 1912: 1; my emphasis);[26] and, again: 'ce *merveilleux* instrument dont le succès sans précédent tient précisément à la variété de ses applications' (Méliès 1912: 2; my emphasis).[27] Similarly, if the documentary side of the equation is predicated on being present at an event in order to capture its unique reality, it is useful to recall that the Lumière brothers reshot the first film, of workers leaving the Lumière factory, three times between 1894 and 1895 (Douchet 1994: 8). Jean-Luc Godard invokes the difficulty of drawing such distinctions in *La Chinoise* (1967) when Jean-Pierre Léaud's character lectures his revolutionary comrades on the fallacy of the dichotomy between Lumière and Méliès.

In the midst of these blurred boundaries, the question arises: If grasping reality is so tricky, how is it possible to tell the truth, or at least to tell the truth from fiction? In the early days of cinema, the truth was something that film alone was not capable of telling. Film was an incomplete medium, which had to be supplemented by something else.

The whole truth and nothing but the truth

André Bazin, discussing the work of Stroheim, once wrote: 'In his films reality lays itself bare like a suspect confessing under the relentless examination of the commissioner of police' (Bazin 1984: 27). Before the invention of intertitles, film did not 'confess' its hidden truths unaided: the services of a *bonimenteur*, or accompanying narrator, were required to shed light on the film's subject, which would reveal itself as if under the glare of police interrogation.[28] But subjects and suspects, be they filmic or judiciary, have been known to 'admit' to things that are not true. There was thus a constant drive to supplement the image – first with speech,

26 'each day brings new inventions, thanks to the *fantastical* development of this industry'.
27 'this *marvellous* instrument, whose unprecedented success stems from the variety of its applications'.
28 Madeleine Malthête-Méliès (1982: 167) affirms that the texts accompanying *L'Affaire Dreyfus* have never been located.

and then, once Méliès invented the serial film, with more images. The series format, which anticipated the vogue for episodic serial films such as Feuillade's *Fantômas* and *Judex*, followed in the nineteenth-century realist tradition of the newspaper *feuilleton*, conveying the breathless impulse to supplement and expand on a story told as if spontaneously: 'This happened, and then this, and then this ...'. If fades, dissolves and irises provide the 'punctuation' between scenes in a modern film, then Méliès's series is a radical form of interfilmic punctuation that anticipated the intrafilmic punctuation that would develop soon afterward, in Méliès's own work as well as in the work of others. The lack of a full stop, or closure, in each of the films in the series as well as in the series as a whole, which ends inconclusively, only reinforces the perceived need for a supplementary voice to impose meaning on the images.

Méliès's images were supplemented by speech, as written accounts of the Dreyfus Affair were supplemented by his film, and as writing is supplemented by speech (albeit speech that is silent to the film viewer) in two of the tableaux within the film. The *bonimenteur* is like a lawyer arguing a case, interpreting evidence, imbuing events with meaning, arranging them into a teleologically coherent narrative. Or like a historian, who makes events that occurred in the past accessible to modern-day readers (or viewers, in the case of televised history programmes), and who provides the discourse which, according to Michel de Certeau, 'suppose un décalage entre l'opacité silencieuse de la "réalité" qu'elle cherche à dire, et la place où elle produit son discours, protégé par une mise à distance de son ob-jet [sic]' (de Certeau 1975: 9).[29] History, like the *bonimenteur*, would present 'une problématique articulant un savoir-dire sur ce que l'autre tait, et garantissant le travail interprétif d'une science ("humaine") par la frontière qui le distingue d'une région qui l'attend pour être connue' (de Certeau 1975: 9).[30]

29 'presupposes a gap between the silent opaqueness of the "reality" that [history] is trying to articulate, and the place where [history] produces its discourse, which is protected by a distancing of its object'.

30 'a problematic that articulates a knowledgeable discourse on what the other does not say, guaranteeing the interpretive work of a ("human") science by the border that distinguishes this work from a region that awaits it in order to be revealed'.

In historical accounts, the subject is temporally absent; in Méliès's re-enactment films, the subject is temporally present (having been plucked from 'current events') but spatially absent (it took place 'there', but we are watching it 'here'). Both historical discourse and the *bonimenteur*'s narrative were conceived as ways of compensating for these absences, but they also produced them.

In the two episodes of Méliès's series that do not feature written discourse (the *Bagarre entre journalistes* and the *Conseil de guerre en séance à Rennes*),[31] spoken discourse serves as an explicit surrogate for the document, as a form of communication that is meant to uncover some truth. In the *Bagarre entre journalistes*, those whose profession it is to put pen to paper substitute canes and umbrellas for their plumes and give voice to their inflammatory opinions. In the trial scene, briefs are replaced by the lawyer's oral argumentation, which is so vigorous that it engenders more of the same, as the judge stands and yells back in reply. Here, speech is associated with violent persuasion, with the opposite of reason; sloppy, impassioned, uncontrolled speech seems to overflow the neat boundaries of reasoned written discourse. Speech is equated with propaganda, and thus possibly with bending the truth, like Doublier's spoken account that accompanied a film which, taken on its own, would have caused no offence. The status of speech in Méliès's films reverses phonocentric assumptions about its authenticity, just as the films themselves question what I will call *photocentric* assumptions about the inherent superiority of unstaged documentary film footage (the 'photo' in photocentrism, of course, being Greek for 'Lumière'). Similarly, an analogy may be drawn between the symbiosis of realism and mise en scène and Hayden White's rejection of the distinction between history as a story that is 'found', and fiction as a story that is 'invented', because, according to White, 'This conception of the historian's task ... obscures the extent to which 'invention' also plays a part in the historian's operations' (White 1973: 6–7). So, while appearing to re-enact history, Méliès was actually making it.

31 These are the titles used in the National Film Archive (British Film Institute) synopsis. Alternatively, these episodes are referred to as *La bataille des journalistes au lycée* and *Le Conseil de guerre à Rennes* in Malthête 1989: 6–8.

What the emphasis on written documents in Méliès's series ultimately heralds is a widening of film's functions beyond entertainment to include its use as both historical and legal document, signalling the encroaching influence of the visual media in representing and transmitting cultural values and ascertainments of truth. In the society of the spectacle, the *bordereau* would be replaced by the Rodney King video. Méliès's series is situated at the border not only between two centuries, but also between two modes of documentary representation.

From writing, film quickly took over the role of creating the illusion of presence. Méliès, ever the magician, made viewers marvel at that illusion in many of his films embracing many genres. The dialectic envisaged by Edgar Morin between Lumière and Méliès must, therefore, be rethought: 'Au réalisme absolu (Lumière) répond l'irréalisme absolu (Méliès). Admirable antithèse qu'eut aimée Hegel, d'où devait naître et se développer le cinéma, fusion du cinématographe Lumière et de la féerie Méliès' (Morin 1956: 58).[32] In fact, the dialectic between realism and 'irréalisme' does not occur between Lumière and Méliès, but is contained in its entirety within Méliès's work. His films revel in this dialectic, as if the magician were always holding up a sign, real or imaginary, with the words: 'Passez Muscades' – Hey presto!

References

Barthes, R. (1994), *Camera Lucida*, trans. Richard Howard, New York, Hill and Wang.

Bazin, A. (1984), *What is Cinema?* vol. I, trans. Hugh Gray, Berkeley, CA, University of California Press.

Benjamin, W. (1989), *Illuminations*, New York, Schocken Books.

Bourgeois, H. (1899), 'Autour du procès', *Le Petit journal*, 7 and 8 Sept.

Buck-Morss, S. (1989), *The Dialectics of Seeing*, Cambridge, MA, MIT Press.

32 'The absolute irrealism of Méliès corresponds to the absolute realism of Lumière. Hegel would have loved this wonderful synthesis, out of which cinema would emerge and develop, the fusion of Lumière's *cinématographe* and Méliès's fantasies.'

De Certeau, M. (1975), *L'Ecriture de l'histoire*, Paris, Gallimard.

Derrida, Jacques (1976), *Of Grammatology*, Baltimore, Johns Hopkins University Press.

Deslandes, J. (1963), *Le Boulevard du cinéma à l'époque de Georges Méliès*, Paris, Editions du Cerf.

Deutelbaum, M. (1979), 'Structural Patterning in the Lumière Films', *Wide Angle* 3:1.

Douchet, J. (1994), 'D'un réalisme l'autre', *Retour vers le réel*, (?), Conseil Général de Seine Saint-Denis.

Dreyfus, A. (1994), *Cinq Années de ma vie*, Paris, La Découverte.

Drouin, Michel (ed.) (1994), *L'affaire Dreyfus de A à Z*, Paris, Flammarion.

Elsaesser, T. (ed.) (1990), *Early Cinema: Space, Frame, Narrative*, London, British Film Institute.

Frazer, J. (1979), *Artificially Arranged Scenes*, Boston, G. K. Hall and Company.

Genette, G. (1987), *Seuils*, Paris, Seuil.

Hammond, P. (1974), *Marvellous Méliès*, London, Gordon Fraser.

Huret, M. (1984), *Ciné actualités*, Paris, Henri Veyrier.

Jeanne, R. and Ford, C. (1961), *Le Cinéma et la presse 1895–1960*, Paris, Armand Colin.

Jenn, P. (1984), *Georges Méliès cinéaste*, Paris, Albatros.

Liszka, J. J. (1996), *A General Introduction to the Semiotic of Charles Sanders Peirce*, Bloomington, Indiana University Press.

Malthête, J. (1981), *Essai de Reconstitution du catalogue français de la Star-Film*, (?), Centre Nationale de la Cinématographie.

—— (1989), 'Les Actualités reconstituées de Georges Méliès', *Archives* 21, mars, Institut Jean Vigo-Cinémathèque Toulouse.

—— (1995), 'Georges Méliès, de la non-fiction à la fiction', *1895* 18, été, special issue: 'Images du réel: la non-fiction en France (1890–1930)'.

—— (1996), *Méliès, images et illusions*, Paris, Exporégie.

—— (1996a), 'Méliès et le conférencier', *Iris* 22, Autumn.

Malthête-Méliès, M. (1973), *Méliès l'Enchanteur*, Paris, Hachette.

—— (1982), 'L'Affaire Dreyfus de Georges Méliès', *Les Cahiers de la Cinémathèque* 35/36, automne, special issue: 'Cinéma et histoire, histoire du cinéma'.

Metz, C. (1968), *Essai sur la signification au cinéma*, vol. 2, Paris, Klincksieck.

Morin, E. (1956), *Le Cinéma ou l'homme imaginaire*, Paris, Les Editions de Minuit.

Sadoul, G. (1947) 'Georges Méliès et la première élaboration du langage cinématographique', *Revue Internationale de la Filmologie* 1, juillet-août, 23–30.

—— (1970), *Georges Méliès*, Paris, Seghers.

Sadoul, G. (ed.) (1947), Special Supplement to *Sight and Sound*, August.

Sand, S. (1994), 'Les sosies cinématographiques de Dreyfus', *L'Affaire Dreyfus et le tournant du siècle*, L. Gervereau and C. Prochasson (eds), Paris, BDIC, 224–7.

White, Hayden (1973), *Metahistory: The Historical Imagination in Nineteenth-Century Europe*, Baltimore, Johns Hopkins University Press.

1 Méliès gets a swelled head in *L'Homme à la tête en caoutchouc*, 1901

2 The Baron wakes from uneasy dreams in *Les Hallucinations du Baron de Munchausen*, 1911

3 Méliès performs a card trick in *Les Cartes vivantes*, 1904

4 Dreyfus holding a letter on Devil's Island in *L'Affaire Dreyfus* (Episode 3, *L'Ile du Diable*), 1899

5 Guards find Henry's suicide note in *L'Affaire Dreyfus* (Episode 5, *Le suicide du colonel Henry*), 1899

6 A rising star in *L'Eclipse du soleil en pleine lune*, 1907

7 State-of-the-art rocket launch in *Le Voyage dans la lune*, 1902

8 A fairy; dangling corpses – two kinds of flying women in *Barbe-bleue*, 1901

9 A soldier gets in over his head in *Le Royaume des fées*, 1903

10 The phantom coach in *Les Quat' cents farces du diable*, 1906

11 The French take a break from working on the Channel Tunnel in *Le Tunnel sous la Manche*, 1907

3

The amazing flying woman

In France at the turn of the twentieth century, flying women were all the rage: they were, quite literally, *dans le vent*. From the success of Mlle Azella, the first 'femme volante' on the trapeze in around 1868, to the crowd-pleasing contortions of Miss Aimée, 'la Mouche humaine', at the end of the century, their popularity had grown in leaps and bounds (Adrian 1988: 22 and 74). At the 1900 *Exposition universelle*, the American dancer Loïe Fuller swirled, twirled and swooped her way into the public imagination, evoking the image of a butterfly and the *art nouveau* style so characteristic of the age.[1] At several theatres and fairgrounds, performers such as Erolyna, Ethéréa ('un ange ou presque' – 'an angel, or almost'), Magneta and Miss Beauty drew audiences who came to marvel at the sight of a woman suspended in mid-air (Deslandes & Richard 1968: 209). The writer and filmmaker Jean Cocteau was moved to compose a poem in 1922 celebrating the flying woman's charms, called 'Miss Aérogyne, femme volante':

> Pigeon vole! Aérogyne
> Elle ment avec son corps
> Mieux que l'esprit n'imagine
> Les mensonges du décor.
> Aérogyne, pigeon vole!

1 '"Un papillon, un papillon!" s'écrie alors le public tandis que Loïe Fuller se met à danser dans un envol de drapé animé par la lueur verte des projecteurs.' ('"A butterfly, a butterfly!" cried the public as Loïe Fuller began to dance in a swirl of fabric, luminous in the spotlight's green glow') (Gourarier 1995: 148).

Rêve, allège le dormeur lourd;
Eloa, dompteuse d'Eole
Dans un océan de velours.[2]

The Aérogyne is both corporeal – a 'corps' opposed to the 'esprit' that contemplates it – and ethereal – the 'rêve' ordered to alleviate the sleeper weighted down with the cares of the world. This flight of fancy, however, is an illusion: the flying woman tells decorative lies with her body. This chapter will explore the nature of this illusion as it is evoked in Méliès's films, while examining the contradictions encompassed by the flying woman as she united opposites in an age of transition.

In the *belle époque*, representations of women as supernatural flying creatures were so widespread that in 1888 Catulle Mendès felt compelled to write that 'La "perversité suprême" est désormais d'être "une femme qui est une femme"'(de Palacio 1993: 56).[3] Most of the women in Méliès's films could not be accused of this supreme perversion, because they are not ordinary women: the majority are something else, somehow other-worldly or ethereal, and almost always associated with magic, either as possessors of magical powers or as objects used by a magician to demonstrate them. A great many of these women appear as winged creatures such as fairies, butterfly-women, celestial bodies in the form of stars or moon goddesses, and the lifeless bodies that float in the air in magic tricks. They are often purely decorative, part of the celestial landscape – bearing asteroids aloft, peeping out of stars, or reclining langorously on a crescent moon – as male explorers carry on with the serious business of discovering new worlds. Or they may strike a classical pose, resembling the Three Graces, draped in flowing robes and posing on a pedestal.

The most visible function of flying women in Méliès's films, of course, was that of sex appeal: they provided an excuse to show young women clad in tights and diaphanous garments. Perhaps

2 'Pigeon, fly! Aerogyne/She lies with her body/Better than the mind can grasp/ The artifice of the set./ Aerogyne, pigeon fly/ Dream, lighten the heavy sleeper/ Eloa, tamer of Eole/ In an ocean of velvet'. Cited in Deslandes and Richard 1968: 211.

3 'The "ultimate perversion" now is to be "a woman who is a woman"'.

not surprisingly, Méliès seems to have envisioned his potential audiences in his own image, composed of male heterosexual viewers who would find the sight of these women especially appealing. If the closest Méliès got to pornography *per se* involved showing Jehanne d'Alcy in a flesh-coloured body stocking being doused with a bucket of water (actually coal dust) in the 1897 *Après le bal – le Tub/After the Ball*, his films, like his stage productions, certainly did project sexualized images of women whenever possible. Méliès also projected such images *wherever* possible, including the wall above the entrance to the Théatre Robert-Houdin. René Jeanne explains that Méliès projected scenes from his films above the entrance in order to attract the public, and that these scenes 'étaient naturellement et astucieusement prises parmi les plus spectaculaires, les plus alléchantes du programme, celles où paraissaient de jolies filles en travesti ou incarnant déesses, nymphes ou fées en maillot académique donnant, à condition qu'on eût beaucoup d'imagination, l'illusion de la nudité' (Jeanne 1965: 120).⁴ The innocence and childishness associated with fairies thus legitimated, made socially acceptable, the voyeurism these figures were used to elicit. However, while sex appeal was clearly one of their explicit functions, these images of flying women also bore a symbolic resonance that went beyond mere titillation.

The ethereal creatures in Méliès's films were usually played by ballet dancers from the companies at the Théâtre du Châtelet or the Folies-Bergère. Classical and other forms of dance had always provided a kind of culturally legitimated voyeurism, allowing spectators to glimpse parts of women's bodies that were not ordinarily exposed in public spaces. Ballerinas – leaping, twirling on tiptoes, or borne aloft by a male partner – would seem to be flying women *par excellence*. But women in Méliès's films do not often move by means of self-propulsion; they appear as part of a still tableau with wings spread, or, if they do move, their

4 'were naturally, and strategically, chosen from the most spectacular and titillating scenes on the programme, those that feature pretty girls dressed as men or goddesses, nymphs, or fairies clad in tutus that gave the illusion of nudity, provided one had enough imagination'.

movement is often governed by photographic and editing tricks. In other words, they are more often than not made to appear and disappear.

If the categories of flying woman and disappearing woman often overlap, it is because they have much in common. Both disappearance and elevation make women appear ethereal or insubstantial. Ethereal, disappearing women are plentiful in Méliès's films, and can be classed in two categories. The first kind is spirited away by a magician or magician figure; the second kind disappears of her own volition in order to thwart the desire of a male.

The first kind of disappearing woman, the kind who is conjured away by a magician, is the most prevalent. In the 1896 *Escamotage d'une dame chez Robert-Houdin/The Vanishing Lady*, the magician makes Jehanne D'Alcy disappear by draping a sheet over her as she sits in a chair. When he attempts to bring her back, a skeleton appears in her place; grimacing, he tries again, and this time succeeds in making her reappear. This film demonstrates that, although the magician's powers sometimes falter and need a bit of adjustment, they eventually prevail, establishing his ultimate control over the woman's existence.

The magician, moreover, is almost always synonymous with the filmmaker. In *Escamotage*, Jehanne D'Alcy's disappearance appears to be attributable to Méliès the magician, but is actually engineered in the editing room by Méliès the filmmaker. Sometimes, the omnipotent magician may play a supporting role in a more elaborate film, such as the 1903 *La Statue animée/The Drawing Lesson*, in which a trickster or magician figure creates the statue of a woman out of ordinary objects – a spinning ball becomes her head, a handkerchief becomes her torso, and the man's own coat becomes the rest of the woman's body. He then disappears, and his rival, a drawing instructor, enters; the 'statue' sneakily swipes the instructor's hat from his head, and then disappears herself without fanfare, no longer required for the film's plot. Although the magician is shown to make the woman appear in the first place, her subsequent disappearance – at the very moment that she demonstrates a will of her own by snatching the drawing teacher's hat – can be attributed to none other than the filmmaker. The filmmaker comes to replace the magician, accomplishing with substitution splicing and multiple exposure the illusions that the magician used to create with trap doors and pulleys before the advent of cinema.

The magician is sometimes shown turning his powers on himself, as both the subject and the object of his own disappearing act. In the 1903 *L'Enchanteur Alcofribas/Alcofribas the Master Magician* (whose name derives from 'Alcofrybas Nasier', an anagram of François Rabelais in *Pantagruel*), a magician puts a woman into a trance, and levitates her before making her disappear. He then conjures up a waterfall, on whose spray three women appear to float before disappearing to make way for a spinning disc of fire in which a larger-than-life woman's face appears (a rare use of close-up for Méliès). The face smiles, then fades out; the magician himself then disappears. While the women in this film are entirely subjected to the magician's control, the magician can turn his magical power on himself whenever he wishes. His disappearance appears as a demonstration of his own subjective agency, whereas the women's role is limited to that of objects used to demonstrate the magician's prowess, made to appear and disappear like rabbits out of a hat.

Similarly, in the 1906 *Les Bulles de savon animées/Soap Bubbles* (also known as *Les Bulles de savon vivantes*) women float, flap their wings and pose, all at the whim of the god-like magician who breathes life into them, and then gets rid of them when he has had enough. The illusionist, played, as ever, by Méliès, first makes a woman appear in a column of smoke, and then blows soap bubbles from a pipe, making women's heads appear and float up to pedestals, where they turn into whole, winged women. Méliès grabs the women, who turn into butterfly kites, which he waves triumphantly before flicking them away. The magician then conjures up three more women who wear classically draped robes and stand in a Three Graces pose on another pedestal; Méliès hops up with them, and they clasp arms, encircling him. He holds out his arms horizontally, and the women fade into oblivion. The magician twirls, bows, and then crouches down and folds his body into a foetal position; a giant soap bubble gradually envelops him as he fades away. As the empty bubble rises into the air, two alarmed male assistants rush in, looking for Méliès, who then returns to surprise them. He laughs and bows.[5] In this film, the disappearance of the women and Méliès's disappearance take on very different meanings. The disappearance of the male magician is presented as cause for alarm, whereas the women's disappearance is taken for granted, as a matter of course. Unlike his female counterparts, Méliès reappears outside of his bubble, feet firmly planted on the ground. What initially appears as a moment of vulnerability on the part of the magician, shown crouching like a foetus in a fragile bubble, reinforces his omnipotence when it turns out to have been a practical joke.

The role of magician in Méliès's films is often played by a diabolical figure. In *Le Chaudron infernal/The Infernal Cauldron* (1903), a devil forces a woman into a big pot, from which then emerge three floating women in the steam, clad in diaphanous garments (whose less-than-graceful movement might be attributed to the fact that they are suspended in the air on wires). They then turn into flames and burn out, after which the devil jumps into the cauldron himself, and evaporates into a puff of steam – presumably in order to join the women. Richard Abel has identified in this film what he calls 'a strongly gendered "beauty of erasure"'(Abel 1998: 65). Similarly, in *La Boîte à malice/The Mysterious Box* (1903), a scientist with magic powers makes a woman disappear into a box before jumping in after her and disappearing himself.

In *Cinematernity*, Lucy Fischer argues that scenarios in which women are made to disappear by a male magician are revenge fantasies, expressions of a jealous desire for retribution on the part of men with womb envy (1996: 47–52). It is certainly true that, in many films, the male magician appropriates the role of reproductive agent; this appropriation is especially evident in

5 It should be noted that Frazer's account does not mention the pipe, the kites, or the fact that Méliès joins the women on the pedestal; and, most significantly, Frazer's account ends with Méliès's disappearance (1979: 171). My own description is based on my viewing of the NFA copy of the film.

films that feature living dolls – inanimate objects into which the magician has breathed life. In *La Statue animée*, as we have seen, a man uses ordinary objects to cobble together the statue of a woman, who then comes to life. Earlier, the man twice strikes a pose reminiscent of a female flamenco dancer or beauty contestant, in anticipation of the female he will soon fashion *ex nihilo*. The male's mimicking of femininity reinforces the procreative nature of his art. This association is emphasized further in films such as *L'Impressionniste fin de siècle/An Up-to-date Conjuror* (1899) and *Illusions Funambulesques/Extraordinary Illusions* (1903), which both begin when a man brings a doll to life, and which both include numerous substitution splices in which Méliès turns into a woman and back again. In the latter film, a magician constructs a life-sized female doll from parts taken from his magical box, and then brings her to life by kissing her: when he later turns into the woman briefly via a substitution splice, he is turning into the very woman he has created, thus becoming both subject and object of procreation. The magician, in other words, gives birth to himself. This desire is also reflected in moments when the magician, here as in *Les Bulles de savon animées*, curls up into a foetal position before disappearing.

It is less clear, however, whether the desire to control reproduction is what motivates the kinds of disappearances described above. These elisions are undoubtedly revenge fantasies, but it is not certain that they are linked causally to the desire for reproductive control. It seems more likely that the motivation for these disappearances is to be found in the frequent occurrence of another kind of disappearing woman in Méliès's films: the beautiful, inaccessible temptress who turns into a frightening creature or disappears altogether as a man attempts to approach her. *L'Escamotage*, as it happens, does not fall into this category, because it ends by demonstrating the complete control that the male magician has over women. Although there is tension built into this early film when Jehanne D'Alcy reappears as a skeleton, Méliès nonetheless succeeds in 'getting the girl' in the end (thus prefiguring the plot of most Hollywood movies: boy meets girl, boy loses girl, boy gets her back). Similarly, in other films such as *Le Chaudron infernal*, if the woman does not return, the magician-devil will join her by disappearing after her, thereby 'getting her back', albeit somewhere else.

But the prospect of losing the woman, which Méliès dangles teasingly in front of viewers before ultimately withdrawing it, is played out in full in films depicting the second kind of disappearing woman, who disappears of her own accord. In these films, the man's vulnerability, which was insincere in *Les Bulles de savon animées*, is genuine. In *Le Monstre/The Monster* (1903), for example, a man, overcome with joy at the sight of his deceased wife who has been revived by a conjurer, reaches out to embrace her, but she returns to skeleton form in his arms. The bereaved husband's horror at the sight of the skeleton recalls the expression on the magician's face when Jehanne D'Alcy reappears as a skeleton in *L'Escamotage d'une dame*. Both images derive from the poetic tradition of *memento mori*, from François Villon's 'Où sont les neiges d'antan', in which the poet reflects on the now-decrepit state of women once famed for their youthful beauty; to Nicolas Poussin's pastoral painting 'Et in Arcadia ego', and then to the poetry of Baudelaire, whose 'La Charogne' details the horrors of rotting female flesh.

Other films by Méliès reinforce the theme of elusive beauty, such as *Bob Kick, L'Enfant terrible/Bob Kick the Mischievous Kid* (1903), in which a ball placed on a table turns into a woman's talking head; when the overgrown child, played by Méliès, tries to kiss the woman's head, it turns into the head of a scowling old man. In *Le Rêve de l'horloger/The Clockmaker's Dream* (1904), a clockmaker tries to embrace a woman in his dreams, but she turns into a giant clock in his grasp. In *Les Quat'cents farces du diable/The Merry frolics of Satan* (1906), a magic pill makes a beautiful fairy materialize, but when William Crackford approaches her, she turns into a monster. In *Le Rêve d'un fumeur d'opium/The Dream of an Opium Fiend* (1908), the moon appears to a hallucinating man as a beautiful woman. When he tries to woo her, she turns into a hideous monster. In *Conte de la grand'mère et rêve de l'enfant/Au Pays des jouets/Grandmother's Story*, also 1908, a little boy dreams that a fairy reveals to him an enchanted garden full of butterfly-women fluttering among the flowers, but when the boy wakes up and attempts to reach for the women, they fade away, and he is left grasping at nothing.[6]

Alternatively, a man's desire may be thwarted when he himself is transformed magically by a powerful woman, as *La Chrysalide et le papillon/The Brahmin and the Butterfly* (1901; also called *Le Brahmane et le papillon*) illustrates. In this film, a man wearing Arabian-style robes and a turban uses flute music, affectionate pats and kisses, and finally bodily force to coax a giant caterpillar into a huge, flip-top cocoon. After a few magical gestures of encouragement, the cocoon pops open and a butterfly-woman emerges, a woman in a striped bodysuit and enormous, swirl-patterned butterfly wings, who floats out and balances for a moment on the hand of the robed man. She then lands on the ground and dances joyfully, fluttering her giant wings, while the man chases her with a blanket. He finally manages to throw the blanket over her as two women in middle-Eastern dress enter. The women remove the blanket to reveal a wingless woman, also in middle-Eastern dress. The two assistants exit, and the man drops to his knees, imploring the former butterfly-woman (for her mercy? her favour?). She shuns him and turns away; as he grabs hold of her flowing headdress, she points at him, transforming him into a giant caterpillar resembling the one from the beginning of the film. She turns her back to the camera and walks off, followed by the other two women who appear again from the left side of the screen, and followed by the caterpillar, which wiggles its hind quarters enthusiastically.[7]

In this film, Méliès mocks the tradition – and, indeed, his own practice – of the male conjuror who makes women appear and disappear and transforms them at whim. In this inverted revenge fantasy, the woman is shown getting the upper hand, with the

6 Descriptions of the two films made in 1908 are based on synopses from Malthête 1981: 297–8 and 324–5.

7 In 1907, Chomón, directing for Pathé, made *Le Charmeur*, which bears a suspicious resemblance to Méliès's earlier *La Chrysalide et le papillon*, the only significant difference being that the butterfly-woman produces five more like her from the chrysalis.

presence of the two other women suggesting a conspiratorial solidarity. As is often the case in Méliès's films, women are shown being cruel to a man, but here their cruelty appears to be motivated. The man seems to have been put in his rightful place, his own desire as subjugated as that of the caterpillar whom he bent to his own will at the beginning of the film, which nonetheless ends on a light note, as the phallic insect's wriggling body indicates that he is still full of drive and vigour. But this film also illustrates that, as long as a woman can float in the air, she can be made to yield to a man's desire; it is only when she comes down to earth (notably, thanks to two other women, who have removed her blanket), that she develops a will of her own.

These scenes suggest that the second type of disappearing woman (in which a woman cruelly eludes a man's grasp) may serve as an intertextual pretext for the first type, discussed by Fischer, in which a woman is conjured out of existence by a man. In other words, if they are shown being subjugated in some films, their portrayal as manipulative, aggressive creatures in other films creates a general representational context that provides justification for their subsequent subjection, as if they were merely being 'paid back' for their unpleasant behaviour. Sometimes, both pretext and punishment are provided in the same film, as in *Le Rêve du maître de ballet/The Ballet Master's Dream* (1903), where the power that women are perceived to have over male sexual desire is shown to provoke a reciprocal desire for mastery: according to the *Essai de Reconstitution* ..., in this film about a 'ravissante danseuse', 'le Maître tente de la saisir entre ses bras, mais elle se transforme en vieille femme grotesque qui le repousse ... Elle vient narguer le Maître qui la renverse sur le lit et la bourre de coups de poings' (Malthête 1981: 166-7).[8] In the next scene, the dance teacher is shown in bed punching his pillow, having dreamt the whole thing. Similarly, *Le Voyage à travers l'impossible/The Impossible Voyage* (1904) contains a scene in which a servant – a woman dressed as a man – is kicked violently

8 'the Master attempts to take her in his arms, but she turns into a hideous old woman who repels him ... She goes to taunt the Master, who throws her onto the bed and pummels her'.

by the inventor of the flying submarine as s/he tries to serve him tea. So, although Méliès sometimes tempers these scenes of retribution through the use of dream sequences and parody, their presence in his work should not be overlooked.

The desire for mastery, the wish to see punished those who threatened to disrupt established social order, was an explicit component of the literary genre from which Méliès's *féeries* ultimately derived: the fairy tale.[9] In his preface to the 1695 edition of *Griselidis, nouvelle, avec le conte de Peau d'Asne et celuy des Souhaits ridicules*, Perrault, whose *Contes de ma Mère l'Oye* codified the French fairy tale genre in the seventeenth century, wrote: 'Quelques frivoles et bizarres que soient toutes ces fables dans leurs avantures, il est certain qu'elles excitent dans les enfans le désir de ressembler à ceux qu'ils voyent devenir heureux, et en mesme temps la crainte des malheurs où les méchans sont tombés par leur méchanceté'.[10] The fairy tale, at least in the French tradition, was meant to educate as well as entertain, providing models of desirable social behaviour to be imitated, as well as examples of behaviour whose repercussions suggested that they were to be avoided.

Like Perrault's tales, Méliès's films reinforced social hierarchies by means of a readily assimilable moral – and, where this moral involved fairies, it often had to do with expectations about women's roles. The flying creatures for whom the *féerie* was named had a far less ambiguous gender identity in France than they did in, for example, Great Britain, where fairies seem to have been male as often as they have been female, or at the very least androgynous (as in Shakespeare's Ariel from *The Tempest*, or Oberon from *A Mid-summer Night's Dream*). In France, fairies had more strictly feminine associations. The *Grand Dictionnaire*

9 The term 'conte des fées' (with the definite article) is thought to have been coined by Mme d'Aulnoy, whose *Contes des fées* was published in 1698; see Opie 1980: 18.

10 'However frivolous and bizarre the adventures depicted in these fables, there is no doubt that they evoke in children the desire to resemble those they see made happy, and the fear of misfortune that is the reward for evil deeds.' Cited in Saintyves 1987: 21.

universel du XIXe siècle, for example, defines a fairy as an '(ê)tre surnaturel, qu'on représente sous la forme d'une femme ... Par ext. Femme remarquable par ses grâces, son esprit ou sa bonté' (1982: 187).[11] This slippage between fairies and women occurred regularly. *La Grande Encyclopédie* offers a potted history of the gender of fairies, a history that seems somehow to have eluded their British cousins: 'Quand la notion du genre neutre disparut, on attribua à ces divinités le sexe masculin ou féminin: mais, comme leur caractère les rapprochait sans doute davantage de la nature féminine, les *fati* ... disparurent assez vite, tandis que les *fatae* passaient dans la mythologie de tous les peuples romains' (vol. 17: 119–20).[12] So, characteristics attributed to 'la nature féminine' influenced representations of fairies, which in turn, through the rewards and punishments meted out in moralistic endings to the tales, reinforced well-established gender roles. Women were shown to conform to these roles even in *féeries* that were ostensibly about women triumphing against the odds. Méliès's 1899 *Cendrillon* and the 1901 *Barbe-bleue* are two of the most notable examples of this pattern.

Like the good fairy in *Le Royaume des fées*, the fairy godmother in the 1899 *Cendrillon* engineers the triumph of good over evil, but the actual extent of her influence is not great. She might seem all-powerful, but upon closer inspection her powers prove to be limited. It is a male imp who makes life difficult for Cinderella, and it is the prince who rescues her from a life of drudgery. The fairy godmother has little more to do than help Cinderella with her wardrobe and transport; otherwise, she can only remind her of the time limit imposed on her by the imp. At the end of the film, the fairy godmother is a resplendent vision of beauty perched atop a spectacular still tableau, mirroring the beautiful but essentially

11 'a supernatural being, represented in the form of a woman; by extension, a woman noted for her grace, her wit, or her kindness'.

12 'When the concept of the neuter gender disappeared, these divinities were divided up into masculine or feminine categories: but, since fairies' attributes were doubtless more feminine in nature, the male *fati* ... quickly disappeared, whereas the female *fatae* entered the mythological systems of all Romanic peoples.' For discussion of the feminine gender of fairies, see also Bernard-Griffiths and Guichardet 1993: 202.

useless role that she has helped Cinderella attain: that, ultimately, of a decorative accessory to male accomplishment.

Barbe-bleue/Blue-beard (1901) ends with a similar visual tableau, over which presides a fairy with spark-like rays emanating from her chest, evoking the contemporary icon known as the *fée électricité*, or electricity fairy. Below her, a hawk-sized dove beats its mechanical wings – a metaphor for the flying woman. But earlier in the film, we are shown a very different kind of airborne woman: the female cadavers dangling from hangman's ropes combine flying (because suspended in the air) woman with disappearing (because lifeless) woman in a portmanteau of sadistic voyeurism, illustrating in an unusually graphic manner the idea that women are easier to control when suspended in mid-air. But at the end of the film, Barbe-bleue is himself killed and the dead women come back to life, able to enjoy their revenge. At first glance, this film would appear to be the ultimate female revenge fantasy, a *Thelma and Louise* of the *belle époque*. But Barbe-bleue is, in fact, killed by a couple of men, while the good fairy can do little more than look on encouragingly: another apparent female revenge fantasy thus breaks down upon close inspection.

Some films, rather than depict punishment (of men or women), provide a reassuring foil in the form of another female figure who 'undoes' the damage caused by the first one. One example of such a 'good cop/bad cop' scenario occurs in *La lune à un mètre/The Astronomer's Dream* (1898), in which the moon, equated through a series of substitutions with Jehanne D'Alcy, devours a hapless astronomer who is then put back together by a benevolent fairy: here, the nightmarish scenario is suggested but subsequently withdrawn (thereby allowing certain viewers to sleep more easily). This depiction of dismemberment and reintegration (the reversal of an infant's perception of its mother as a conglomeration of part-objects) would, in the classic psychoanalytic scenario, represent the threat of castration followed by its disavowal, its imaginary overcoming in a phantasmatic plenitude (see Williams 1986: esp. 525–7). The phallic metaphor is not particularly subtle here: the male points his telescope at the moon, but it collapses; then, when he tries a longer telescope, the moon takes a bite out of it. When the moon goddess appears before him, he tries to embrace her, but she rises up and away into the air, true to form as the disappearing temptress. The woman is then shown again, dressed differently, reclining on the crescent moon, before being replaced by the headless statue of a man (prefiguring the dismemberment to come) which is in turn transformed into a huge moon face that gobbles up the astronomer before spitting him out. In one shot, Jehanne d'Alcy as Phoebe the moon goddess lounges alluringly on the crescent moon; a substitution splice then turns the moon into a menacing ball that devours the astronomer. The implication seems to be that, as long as she is up in the air, unattainable, the woman poses no threat; but once she comes within arm's reach, she will cause harm.

As Linda Williams has noted, 'Even when women's bodies do not appear at all [in Méliès's films], the threat of castration posed by their bodies seems to underlie the pattern of each scenario' (Williams 1986: 527). In Méliès's films, the female body is thus shown to be as frightening as it is fascinating. Méliès went on to develop this theme in subsequent films, culminating in the 1903 *Royaume des fées*, his most lavish production to date, which merits close analysis, as it dramatizes the anxieties surrounding feminine sexuality with particularly insistent symbolic force.

Le Royaume des fées/The Kingdom of the Fairies (1903)

The story is loosely based on the ballet *Biche au Bois*, first presented at the old Porte Saint-Martin in 1845 (Frazer 1979: 6–7). In this film, a man embarks upon a treacherous rite of initiation into the world of feminine sexuality by means of an elaborate series of reproductive metaphors. The film opens at the court of the King, who, from the height of his raised throne, blesses the marriage proposal of a prince (played by Méliès – at 42, remarkably agile – in puffy doublet, tights and shoulder-length wig) to his daughter the princess. As the happy couple sit down for a chat with the King and Queen, an evil witch, dressed in a shapeless brown costume reminiscent of a monk's robes, runs in from the right and curses the prince and princess. (Abel describes this character as a male, but the American Star-Film catalogue confirms that it is a female witch (Méliès 1905: 27).) The prince begs the witch for mercy, then takes out his sword and attacks her, and she disappears in flames. The evil witch is a woman past child-bearing age who is presumably jealous of the couple's happiness.

In the next scene, the princess enters her lavishly appointed sleeping quarters accompanied by her ladies in waiting, who remove her outer garments and help her slip into her nightclothes. She climbs into bed, whose design and trim resemble a giant sea-shell (a conventional sexual metaphor), and the ladies in waiting, whose pointy renaissance hats and aprons are reminiscent of the costumes worn in Alice Guy's 1899 *Fée aux choux*, exit. As the princess settles in for a night's sleep, the witch appears with her goblin assistants, who scoop up the slumbering princess and carry her off in a chariot. The prince runs in, sword drawn, to do battle with a lingering goblin – but as phallic objects make ineffective arms in the absence of the beloved, the goblin eludes the prince, disappearing in a puff of smoke. The prince runs after the chariot and the pyjama-clad king and queen enter, followed by a crowd of ladies-in-waiting and various sleepy servants brandishing mops and feather dusters, more limply ineffective metaphors.

Later in the film, the evil witch appears before the prince as he prepares for battle, and shows him a magical vision of the princess being hoisted over a castle wall by the witch's evil minions. Her dangling body, suspended by a rope, recalls the scene in *Barbe-bleue* that shows seven female cadavers hanging from the ceiling; both images fall under the 'helpless appendage' category of flying woman. The prince raises his sword against the witch, but she beats him to it and conks him on the head with her cane before hopping up the stairs on a broomstick (reminding us that she is a threatening sort of flying woman). But as the prince lies wounded on the floor, a good fairy appears brandishing a flowered sceptre with which she taps the prince, undoing the damage caused by the witch. Once again, the reassuring variety of flying woman has saved the day – but we can be certain that the witch will strike again, as we see her running onto the dock from which the prince has set sail, cursing and waving her arms furiously.

After encountering a storm, the ship sinks to the bottom of the sea, a fantastical landscape crowded with lush plantlife and women swimming past, suspended on ropes, as a hyperactive octopus wriggles its legs vigorously – more phallic metaphors. A chariot drawn by a large fish with flapping fins glides in from the left and a fairy alights; as the chariot slips back out of the frame, she gently pokes at the sea bed with her long sceptre, reviving inanimate lumps that are now revealed to be the shipwrecked heroes, who awaken and embrace each other. In the film's on-going sexual odyssey, the fairy's prodding has managed to get a rise out of the lethargic prince and his men, but there still lies trouble ahead. The fairy exits to the left and the men stagger after her. A dissolve reveals a rocky, underwater grotto, with more swimming women floating past from left to right, followed by the fairy driving her fish-drawn chariot. Behind her, the prince rides a giant swordfish, which stalls; he spurs and whips it, but has still not managed to restart it when the scene cuts to another. The prince's initial difficulty, however, seems to have been overcome when a series of multi-layered moving backdrops of tangled oceanic flora and fauna give way – prefiguring the filmic technique of the wipe – to reveal a watery cave filled with dentata-like stalactites descending almost to the floor. This backdrop, too, rises to reveal yet another, giving the impression that the prince and his men are penetrating ever further into the depths of the cave. There, the men encounter the Queen of the Deep, who lends them the use of a giant whale to transport them to the castle in which the princess is being held prisoner. As the whale deposits the men on land through its open mouth, real water is ejaculated from its blow-hole, as if to confer a metonymic potency on the prince. It is then without difficulty (though with a bit more help from the good fairy) that he rescues the princess from the burning castle and throws the witch over a cliff in a barrel.

In the triumphant homecoming – an uncharacteristic long shot apparently filmed on the grass outside Méliès's studio at Montreuil – the princess is greeted by the King and a crowd of courtiers as she is carried on a litter; behind her, the prince rides in triumphantly on his horse, which is much more obedient than the swordfish he attempted to ride in the kingdom beneath the sea. A dissolve brings a cloud-painted set that parts – a theatrical technique prefiguring the filmic effect of the iris – to reveal the palace interior, while a woman wearing long white robes waves her arms in the middle of the frame and steps into the background, as if to bid the set to open further and welcome viewers into the scene (and, presumably, to welcome the prince into the princess's body – passage through this cloud-painted set appears smoother than through the tangle of marine vegetation encountered earlier). The film's final tableau shows the ecstatic prince and modestly bashful princess surrounded by nine cradles.

Le Royaume des fées, in effect an elaborate fertility rite, thus depicts the successful initiation of a man into the perceived mysteries of feminine sexuality. The evil, old witch, long past child-bearing age, is juxtaposed with the beautiful young fairy guide, who triumphs at every turn. The many images of grottos, caves and shells suggest female sexual organs, whereas the giant swordfish that refuses to do the prince's bidding is an unmistakable metaphor for male impotence. The sperm whale that carries the prince and his men on the road to sexual potency is an all-purpose image of sexual polymorphousness: it swallows the men, spewing forth water in a great stream out of its blow hole, before 'giving birth' to them on the rocky shore. The nine infants that appear in the film's final image are the prince's bountiful reward for successfully negotiating the deep waters of female sexuality, presented as a threatening alterity. Even the film's theatrical precursor was associated with an intimidating feminine sexuality: the dancer Lola Montès had provoked a scandal when she performed in *La biche au bois* in 1845, 'en paraissant en scène sans maillot, les jambers nues' (Sadoul 1970: 53).[13]

As Lucy Fischer writes of the disappearing women in Méliès's films, 'the act of conjuring and "vanishing" ladies tends to *dematerialize and decorporealize the female sex*, to relegate women

---

13 'appearing on stage without a leotard, in bare legs'.

to the level of "spirit."'(Fischer 1996: 41; original emphasis). Her assertion that the female sex in Méliès's films is decorporealized must, however, be qualified in light of the films discussed above: women are represented in Méliès's films as transcendental through the very materiality of their bodies. The ethereal, spiritual quality attributed to these figures is in fact an *alibi* for the stark materiality to which they are reduced as fetish objects. Méliès is trying to make women's bodies seem less threatening, while at the same time, giving viewers the opportunity to take a good, long look.

Conquering polarities

At the turn of the century, women's roles were changing – or, at least, were perceived by many to be changing – and the anxieties that these changes provoked were both reflected and problematized in film, and in the culture at large, in the overdetermined image of the flying woman. At the Atheneum Theatre, a *fête foraine* nicknamed 'the Aérogyne' after its most famous attraction, the flying woman, was billed with two other attractions: 'Les Visions Lumineuses Aériennes', or a display of the new technological marvel electricity, and 'Le Biographe en Couleurs', which was an American-built camera-projector that screened hand-tinted films (Deslandes and Richard 1968: 179). These three cultural obsessions – flying women, technological advancement, and the new medium of cinema – converged not only at the Aérogyne, but also in Méliès's longest film (at 650 metres, or roughly thirty minutes), which was also one of his last: *A la conquête du Pôle/The Conquest of the Pole* (1912), considered by some to be his finest work. Georges Sadoul, for example, has written: 'Peut-être jamais ne réalisa-t-il d'oeuvre plus parfaite que sa *Conquête du Pôle* ' (Sadoul 1970: 75).[14]

The opposition that the film sets up initially takes the form of a rivalry between the sexes, but ultimately develops into a dicho-

---

14 '*A la conquête du Pôle* is perhaps his most perfect creation'.

tomy between two representations of a single sex, in other words, between two variants of flying woman. In the film's opening scenes, which recall the filmmaker's 1902 *Voyage dans la lune*, a group of male explorers are designing a flying machine that will take them to the North Pole.[15] Their preparations are interrupted when a group of scowling, trouser-clad women, whose leader is a caricature of the British suffragette Emmeline Sylvia Pankhurst, arrives on the scene with placards bearing inscriptions such as 'Délégation des suffragettes', 'Aux femmes le Pôle', 'Le Pôle aux femmes', and 'Nous voulons aller au Pôle. A bas les hommes.'[16] The intertitle announcing this scene is labelled, 'Une délégation de suffragettes tente inutilement de troubler les sévères travaux du Congrès'.[17] When the group leader is unable to start her vehicle, a large sled with small party balloons pasted all over it, she jumps out and uses her belly to shove a man who attempts to usher her out, and storms off, leaving the much smaller man to writhe on the ground. She is accompanied by female assistants dressed in sailor suits and Napoleon hats. We next see her attempting to climb aboard the aerobus containing most of the male explorers, but a bilingual sign with the words 'Complet/Full' is hastily hung over the door, and the woman is wrested away by three policemen. After knocking over a couple of men who try to get in her way, she attempts to join another explorer, who has also been left behind, by jumping onto the side of his hot-air balloon as it rises into the sky.[18]

The image of a would-be female aviator was no fantastical

15 The North Pole had been reached by the American Robert E. Peary on 6 April 1909, and the South Pole had been reached by the Norwegian Roald Amundsen on 14 December 1911, just four months before Méliès began filming *A la conquête du Pôle*.

16 'Delegation of suffragettes'; 'To women belongs the Pole'; 'The Pole belongs to women'; 'We want to go to the Pole. Down with men'. These signs do not figure in the US version of this film; this information appears in Malthête 1981: 347.

17 'A delegation of suffragettes tries in vain to disrupt the important proceedings of the Congress'. This intertitle has been cut from the American version of the film, but is signalled in Malthête 1981: 347.

18 For a discussion of derogatory depictions of suffragettes in American film of the first two decades of the twentieth century, as well as of positive depictions in films made by suffragettes themselves, see Sloan 1988 Ch 5.

invention from science fiction, but instead a reflection of the headlines of the day. The origins of women's aviation are located in France: the first woman in the world to fly solo was the French woman Thérèse Peltier, and the first woman to qualify for a pilot's license, Elise de Laroche (first solo flight: 1909; license awarded in 1910), was also French (Boase 1979: 10–11). Moreover, Méliès's representation of the female aviator as a suffragette evokes a similarly topical issue. French women did not gain the right to vote until after the Second World War. Universal suffrage was a contemporary issue when Méliès began making *A la conquête du Pôle* in 1911: the *Union française pour le suffrage des femmes* had been established in 1909, just three years before Méliès's film appeared, and the women's suffrage movement gained great political momentum in the years preceding the First World War.[19] Not surprisingly, universal suffrage was perceived as a threat to male political dominance.[20] There can be no doubt that women's increasing visibility in the political arena – if only, up until then, as protestors of their exclusion from it – was becoming a cause for concern, however latent. Lucy Fischer's remarks about the women who are made to disappear in Méliès's films are best understood in this social context: 'Perhaps the male magician is not only performing tricks upon the female; he is preventing her from performing more dangerous tricks upon him' (Fischer 1996: 45). Indeed, Méliès puts the determined aviatrix in her place, thus preventing her from ever again performing tricks of any kind: after a struggle, she is pushed from the hot-air balloon onto which she has jumped, and falls through the sky, landing spread-eagled on a pointy spire in the town below, where she explodes in a puff of smoke. In one swift motion, Méliès has eradicated the nagging problem of women who demand the same opportunities as men. By ending up impaled through the pelvis, the suggestion is, this woman is getting what she may have needed all along.

19 See Reynolds (1996: 204–21) for a detailed analysis of the suffragist movement in this period.
20 See Rosanvallon 1992: 402; and Huard 1991: 194–210 ff., for a discussion of the development of the female suffrage movement in France from the 1880s to the eve of the First World War.

To this negative image of aggressive aviatrixes, *A la conquête du Pôle* presents an alternative: the celestial flying woman, who appears in the guise of the moon goddess, star-women, and star-bearing fairies (the distinctions among these categories being somewhat fluid). These celestial creatures also appear in *Voyage dans la lune*, watching over the space explorers from above as they sleep off their jet lag on the surface of the moon, and in a galactic fantasia sequence in *Les Quat'cents farces du diable/The Merry Frolics of Satan* (1906), in which women bearing stars float past William Crackford's hallucinatory coach as the explorer blows kisses at them and tries to poke them with his umbrella. A drawing made by Méliès for *A la conquête du Pôle* shows an airplane flying past a planet with a ring around it, beside which float six women holding up stars.[21] The inclusion of these "femme-étoiles" in a drawing characterized by its economy of expression is notable, considering that these creatures only appear in the film very briefly, and suggests that their iconographic status was disproportionate to their screen time. Unlike the thoroughly modern women who attempted to power flying machines of their own and who, though often thwarted in their efforts, signalled both changing technology and women's changing social roles, the celestial flying creatures in *A la conquête du Pôle* were the vestiges of another age. A large part of their charm and their humour derived from their juxtaposition with the trappings of modernity.

The uses of disenchantment

The tradition from which the marvellous flying creatures evolved, the past that was being self-consciously evoked in opposition to all that was modern, was that of the theatrical *féerie* or fantasy play. There was a certain historical logic to the proliferation of fairies and other fantastical flying creatures in Méliès's films, many of which descended directly from the *féeries* that had attracted large

21 This drawing was published posthumously in *Nouvelles littéraires* (24 janvier 1963).

audiences in France since the sixteenth century, when Catherine de Médicis brought over Italian troupes to entertain the court.[22] The heyday of the French *féerie* was in the early nineteenth century, with Martainville's *Pied de Mouton*, which premiered at the Gaîté on 6 December 1806, drawing huge audiences, followed by Laurent and Anicet-Bourgeois's *Les Pilules du Diable* in 1839. Both *féeries* would remain popular throughout much of the nineteenth century, spawning scores of comparable works. Similarly, the publishing world witnessed a boom in fairy tales in the second half of the century: between 1842 and 1913, 233 editions of Perrault's *Contes de ma Mère l'Oye* (Mother Goose Tales) were published by sixty different publishers in France (de Palacio 1993: 22).

But, despite their popularity, by the end of the nineteenth century both fairies and the *féerie* had become the quaint artefacts of an earlier age (see Ginisty 1910: 217; de Palacio 1993). And, like the *féeries* from which they derived, Méliès's later films were already outmoded at the moment of their creation. In 1951, Georges Sadoul wrote:

> 'A la Conquête du Pôle' est aujourd'hui un chef d'oeuvre qui a la perfection d'un Giotto. Mais c'est un Giotto terminé au temps de Michel-Ange et de Raphael. Pour comprendre que ce film admirable rencontra un insuccès presque total, il faut se souvenir qu'il fut presque contemporain de 'Fantômas', de 'Quo Vadis?', des premiers films d'Ince et de Griffith ... Ce créateur en 1898 de l'art du film était en 1912 un attardé (cited in Malthête 1981: 351).[23]

Even at the beginning of Méliès's film career, allusions to the marvellous were already parodic. As early as 1888, Théodore de Banville had written in *Les Belles Poupées* of the impossibility of believing in fairies in the age of electricity:

22 See Ginisty 1910: 12 ff.
23 '"A la conquête du Pôle" [sic] is, today, a masterpiece of the calibre of a Giotto. But it's a Giotto completed in the age of Michaelangelo and Raphael. In order to comprehend how this wonderful film could meet with such failure, we must remember that it was more or less contemporary with "Fantômas", "Quo Vadis?", and the first films by Ince and Griffith. The man who, in 1898, was the creator of the art of cinema was, in 1912, behind the times.'

THE AMAZING FLYING WOMAN 111

– ... contez-nous quelque chose, par exemple un conte de fées.

– Oui, dit monsieur Roman ... mais un conte de fées laïque, c'est-à-dire dans lequel il n'y ait pas de fées. Car, dans le siècle des torpilleurs et de la lumière électrique, nous ne saurions admettre les superstitions abolies, ni rien qui suppose une impossible dérogation aux lois naturelles (de Palacio 1993: 18).[24]

The suggestion is that fairies stretched the boundaries of all but the most carefully suspended disbelief to impossible limits. How, then, to explain their enormous popularity, precisely at the moment when people had ceased to believe in them? Through their strong association with nature (making their homes in woodland haunts, meadows and streams, trees, flowers, and rainbows – to the extent that they were often shown blending almost imperceptibly in to their natural environment, as in Méliès's 1908 *Conte de la grand'mère et rêve de l'enfant/Grandmother's Story* (also called *Au Pays des jouets*), in which butterfly fairies merge with the flowers that surround them), fairies fulfilled a nostalgic function in an age in which France was changing from a predominantly rural, agrarian society to an industrialized, urban one. The industrial revolution reached France later than Britain and the United States, and, at the beginning of the twentieth century, the French populace was still coming to terms with the changes to their way of life.

However, this nostalgia for an earlier era was coupled with an enthusiasm for the scientific marvels of the new century, resulting in a profound ambivalence toward technological and social change. This ambivalence is reflected in the somewhat overdetermined figure of the *fée-électricité* (electricity fairy) . In his memoir *1900*, Paul Morand waxes lyrical about the electricity fairy's presence at the 1900 Exposition universelle:

C'est alors que retentit un rire étrange, crépitant, condensé: celui de la Fée Electricité. Autant que la Morphine dans les boudoirs de 1900, elle triomphe à l'Exposition; elle naît du ciel, comme les

24 '"... tell us a story – a fairy tale". "Yes", said Mister Novel, "but a secular fairy tale, that is, in which there are no fairies. For, in the age of torpedo ships and electric light, we cannot allow outdated superstitions, or anything that presupposes an impossible contravention of natural laws"'.

vrais rois. Le public rit des mots: Danger de mort, écrits sur les pylônes ... Elle est le progrès, la poésie des humbles et des riches; elle prodigue l'illumination; elle est le grand Signal; elle écrase, aussitôt née, l'acétylène. A l'Exposition, on la jette par les fenêtres. Les femmes sont des fleurs à ampoules. Les fleurs à ampoule [singular/plural inconsistency is Morand's] sont des femmes ... Les ministères de la rive gauche, eux-mêmes, ont l'air de Loïe Fullers ... L'Electricité ... c'est le fléau, c'est la religion de 1900. (Morand: 68–69)[25]

Like the flying woman in Méliès's films, the electricity fairy is both ethereal – 'elle naît du ciel' – and deadly – 'danger de mort'; at once menacing – 'elle écrase – and objectified – 'on la jette par les fenêtres', she is associated with both nature and technology ('fleurs à ampoules').

Similarly, Jules Trousset, in *Les Merveilles de l'Exposition de 1900*, which predated the exposition by one year, also represented electricity as a fairy: 'La véritable souveraine de l'Exposition de 1900 sera l'Electricité, cette jeune et brillante fée qui dote l'industrie contemporaine des deux facteurs principaux: le mouvement et la lumière' (Toulet 1986: 180).[26] Movement and light were both powerful forces on their own, but even more so when combined in the new medium of film. Electricity was the clean, modern technology that promised to insulate the French public in a cocoon of scientific progress, warding off danger – whether it was the danger of savagery, averted in Jules Verne's *20,000 Leagues Under the Sea* when Captain Nemo activates the electric fence around the Nautilus to keep out the hoardes of angry

25 'Then a strange, crackling, shrill laugh could be heard: that of the Electricity Fairy. Like Morphine in fin-de-siècle boudoirs, she triumphs at the Exhibition; she hails from the heavens, like true kings. The public laughs at the words 'Danger of death' written on pylons ... She is progress, poetry to rich and poor alike; she spreads illumination; she is the great Signal; she snuffs out acetylene as soon as she is born. At the Exhibition, they throw her out of windows. Women are flower-lights. Flower-lights are women. Even the ministers of the Left Bank seem like so many Loïe Fullers ... Electricity is the scourge and the religion of 1900.'

26 'The true supreme ruler of the 1900 Exhibition will be Electricity, the brilliant young fairy who endows modern industry with two important features: movement and light.'

Papuans, or the very real danger of primitive technology, such as the oxygen-ether used in the projection of early films, which caused the devastating fire at the Bazar de la Charité in 1897, in which over 120 people died. So when in *A la conquête du Pôle* the intertitle leading into the factory scene says, 'L'usine électrique où le professeur Mabout a réalisé son oeuvre' ('the electricity-powered factory where Professor Maboul made his creation'), it is boasting of a brave new world. The adoption of the fairy as an icon of the new technological marvel served, at least in part, to signal what it was that electricity was replacing.

Marcel Mauss has argued that technology plays a role in society similar to that played by magic in earlier times. Automation, he implies, is the modern incarnation of magic: in *A General Theory of Magic*, Mauss places magic 'between' religion and science or technology (1972: 86). He writes: 'magic tends to resemble technology, as it becomes more individualistic and specialized in pursuit of its varied aims. Nevertheless, these two series of facts contain more than an external similarity: there is a function identity, since ... both have the same aims ... Magic is the domain of pure production, *ex nihilo*. With words and gestures it does what techniques achieve by labour' (Mauss 1972: 141). The *fée-electricité* would thus be a hybrid sign of the passage from magic to science, in an era that marked the transition from manual to automated production in the industrial sphere. If fairies initially served to give a face to magic (according to Mauss (1972: 80), 'demons, spirits, etc. are personifications of magical functions'), they were eventually used to give a face to technology, as the belief in magic gave way to an equally unquestioning faith in the power of technology.

It was largely through automation that traditional gender roles were becoming less rigidly defined. Tom Gunning has suggested an evocative analogy between the newly automated manufacturing techniques and the sudden transformations wrought by substitution splicing in early film – transformations that, as we have seen, more often than not involved women: 'the phantasmagoria of the trick film with its magical metamorphoses echoes the transformation of raw material into products achieved nearly instantaneously through the rapid succession of tasks in the new factory system' (Charney & Schwartz 1995: 16). Automation threatened to make the labour market more of a level playing field because it made work no longer so dependent on physical strength. Women were gaining access to many activities, in both the labour and leisure spheres, that had once been closed to them. The workers who hand coloured Méliès's films frame by frame, for example, were all women. And women are shown working in the factory scene in *A la conquête du Pôle*, sewing material for the airplane's frame, like the film editors and colorists whose work resembled the traditionally 'feminine' tasks of quilting and dying garments. It is perhaps also worth noting that in the Lumière brothers' first film, *La Sortie d'usine*, the vast majority of the workers shown leaving the factory are women. Yet, as the work of Siân Reynolds has shown, technology's promises of accessibility – 'Even a slip of a girl can fly it', claimed advertisements for the new airplanes – were not matched by a social willingness to see traditional gender roles change (Reynolds 1996: 65–82). So although there were suffragettes, women trying to fly, they were often – as illustrated in *A la conquête du Pôle* – pushed down just as they were beginning their ascent.

At the turn of the century, the ideal French woman, as embodied in the figure of the fairy, resembled her British counterpart, the Victorian 'angel in the house'. These domestic goddesses were praised for their tendency to fly to men's aid, always helping others, while remaining selfless, good-natured, and otherwise devoid of ambition, as Joséphin Péladan explained in *Comment on devient fée* , an 1893 'how-to' manual that devoted considerable space to explaining 'how-not-to': "'[...] tu ne saurais être ni philosophe, ni poète, ni artiste, ni savante [...]. Et on pourrait bannir des bibliothèques et des musées l'effort féminin, sans y faire un vide"' (cited in de Palacio 1993: 71; all in italics, original ellipses).[27] Both the angel in the house and the French filmic fairy were, above all, helpmeets who enabled men to reach

---

27 '... you could never be a philosopher, a poet, an artist, or a scientist (...). And we could eliminate the entire female contribution from libraries and museums without any great loss'.

greater heights (such as those ushering the plane along in *A la conquête du Pôle*, or the women in sailor suits who launch the rocket in *Voyage dans la lune*).

Nina Auerbach has written that, 'In contrast to her swooping ancestors, the angel in the house is a violent paradox with overtones of benediction and captivity. Angelic motion had once known no boundaries; the Victorian angel is defined by her boundaries' (Auerbach 1982: 72). Méliès's feminine icons, too, were defined by their boundaries. In serving as allegorical figures of nostalgia for an earlier age, fairies also functioned as icons of a conception of femininity that was coming to be challenged in the face of changing gender roles. For the first decades of the twentieth century marked the birth of a new kind of flying woman who rivalled the first kind – those who, unlike the angel in the house, ventured out of the home; those who not only helped men, but also helped themselves.

References

Abel, R. (1998), *The Ciné Goes to Town*, Berkeley, CA, University of California Press.

Adrian, (P.?) (1988), *Ils donnent des ailes au cirque*, Paris, Paul Adrian.

Auerbach, N. (1982), *Woman and the Demon: The Life of a Victorian Myth*, Cambridge, MA, Harvard University Press.

Bernard-Griffiths, S. and Guichardet, J. (eds.) (1993), *Images de la magie. Fées, enchanteurs et merveilleux dans l'imaginaire du XIXe siècle*, Paris, Diffusion les Belles Lettres.

Boase, W. (1979), *The Sky's the Limit: Women Pioneers in Aviation*, London, Osprey Publishing Ltd.

Charney, L. and Schwartz, V. (eds.) (1995), *Cinema and the Invention of Modern Life*, Berkeley, CA, University of California Press.

De Palacio, J. (1993), *Les Perversions du merveilleux: Ma Mère l'Oye au tournant du siècle*, Paris, Séguier.

Deslandes, J. and Richard, J. (1968), *Histoire comparée du cinéma* vol. II, (? Belgium), Casterman.

Fischer, L. (1996), *Cinematernity*, Princeton, Princeton University Press.

Frazer, J. (1979), *Artificially Arranged Scenes*, Boston, G. K. Hall and Company.

Ginisty, P. (1910), *La Féerie*, Paris, Louis Michaud.

Gourarier, Z. (1995), *Il était une fois la fête foraine*, Paris, Editions de la Réunion des musées nationaux.

Grand Dictionnaire universel du XIXe siècle (1982), vol. VIII, Paris, Administration du grand dictionnaire universel; originally published in 1872.

Jeanne, R. (1965), *Cinéma 1900*, Paris, Flammarion.

Malthête, J. (1981), *Essai de Reconstitution du catalogue français de la Star-Film*, (?), Centre Nationale de la Cinématographie.

Mauss, M. (1972), *A General Theory of Magic*, trans. Robert Brain, London, Routledge and Kegan Paul.

Méliès, G. (1905), *Complete Catalog of Genuine and Original 'Star' Films*, New York, Georges Méliès (in BiFi Fonds Méliès GM011).

Morand, P. (1931), *1900*, Paris, Flammarion.

Opie, I. and P. (1980), *The Classic Fairy Tales*, St. Albans, Granada.

Reynolds, S. (1996), *France Between the Wars: Gender and Politics*, London, Routledge.

Rosanvallon, P. (1992), *Le sacre du citoyen*, Paris, Gallimard.

Sadoul, G. (1970), *Georges Méliès*, Paris, Seghers.

Saintyves, P. (1987), *Les contes de Perrault et les récits parallels*, Paris, Robert Laffont.

Sloan, K. (1988),*The Loud Silents: Origins of the Social Problem Film*, Urbana, University of Illinois Press.

Toulet, E., 'Le cinéma à l'Exposition universelle de 1900', *Revue d'histoire moderne et contemporaine*, vol. 33, April–June 1986: 180.

Williams, L. (1986), 'Film Body: An Implantation of Perversions', in Rosen, *Narrative, Apparatus, Ideology*, New York, Columbia University Press, 1986, 507–34. (Originaly published in *Ciné-Tracts* vol. 3, no. 4, Winter 1981: 19–35).

4

Imaginary voyages

As we have seen in previous chapters, Méliès's films transported viewers to other worlds; only some of his films, however, actually emphasized the process of getting there. If movement was the feature of film that set it apart from photography and painting, then it was also the key factor in the development of the tourism industry, and in the transportation revolution inaugurated by the invention of the automobile and the airplane. The transportation revolution made the world a smaller place, and facilitated encounters between people who might not otherwise meet. These encounters were thematized in Méliès's voyage films, which combined magic and fantasy with the new and very real social possibilities presented by developing technologies of motion.

In his first years of production, Méliès made a number of single-scene films that depicted travel in one way or another. *Combat naval en Grèce/Naval Combat in Greece* (1897) is set aboard a ship in the Greco-Turkish War; *Entre Calais et Douvres/Between Calais and Dover* (1897), also set on a ship's deck, shows passengers being tossed about in stormy seas; and the 1898 *Panorama d'un train en marche/Panorama from the Top of a Moving Train*, in which a camera placed atop a speeding train gives viewers the impression of travelling themselves, predates the Hale's Tours 'train cinema' by six years. However, it was only after Méliès developed films with multiple tableaux in 1899 that he could make what we would now recognize as voyage films, which conveyed a sense of departure and return (or, at least, journey's end).

Paul Hammond has noted that 'Méliès was among the first to explore the imagery of *arrival and departure*, in a series of 1896 films photographed à la Lumière: *Arrival of a Train in Vincennes Station, Boat Leaving the Harbour at Trouville* and *Automobile Starting on a Race*. Like a number of contemporary painters (Monet, Pissarro, Seurat and Marquet), the early film-makers turned to the city streets, harbours, railway termini and rivers for their imagery. It was there that things *moved*' (Hammond 1974: 117; original emphasis). Film is a spectator sport, by means of which viewers are transported visually to places they themselves, by their very presence at the film screening, are not going; the mobility of the camera that records the faraway places depicted in the film both gives rise to and compensates for the spectators' own inertia. Méliès never forgot the amazement he felt at taking his first glimpse of a film, which depicted a train pulling into a station; in many of his own films, he would try to replicate that initial wonder. Méliès was among the first to recognize film's capacity to render other worlds accessible to all. Yet, unlike the Lumières, who sent camera operators all over the world to film newsreels and exotic scenes, Méliès shot most of his films at his studio in Montreuil. Most of the mobility in Méliès's films occurred in front of the camera, which, itself, was relatively immobile. But this did not stop Méliès from depicting the most outrageous flights of fancy, as if his voyage films were compensating for the camera's immobility. The motto of the Star-Film company was, after all, 'le monde à la portée de la main' (the world at your fingertips): for Méliès, the 'world' was in large part an imaginary one – although it would become increasingly influenced by real-world events as the years wore on.

The *belle époque* was an era marked by rapid industrialization in France. As industry needed to expand geographically and reach ever wider markets in order to make a profit, it also needed to find ways of saving time. With the spread of wage labour in the nineteenth century and its confirmation as the norm in the twentieth, time became money, whether one was selling or buying. Covering distances in a shorter and shorter period of time thus became increasingly desirable, and inventors sought ever new ways of demonstrating the superiority of technology over nature. Méliès satirized this emphasis on speed and efficiency in *Le Raid Paris-Monte Carlo en deux heures/An Adventurous Automobile Trip* (1905) – even today, an automobile journey of this length could not be completed in the time indicated in the film's title – in which a speeding car flattens passers-by, overturns market stalls, and crashes through buildings left and right. Similarly, the parade of ridiculous vehicles in *A la conquête du Pôle/The Conquest of the Pole* (1912), as well as the inventor William Crackford's predilection for passenger trains that double as hand luggage in *Les Quat'cents farces du diable/The Merry Frolics of Satan* (1906), are parodies of the desperate desire to design ever-more efficient machines to propel people across the globe.

As the title of *A la conquête du Pôle* suggests, much of the travel in Méliès's films had to do with conquering the unknown. The late nineteenth century witnessed the most frenetic imperial expansion the world had ever known, as Britain and France subjected huge areas of the globe to their colonial rule. The changing times brought changes to traditional ways of life that, like traditional assumptions about the order of the world, were becoming obsolete. In Méliès's voyage films, the old world is shown in confrontation with the new; the inevitable collisions depicted in these films – the smashing of cars into buildings, the crash landings of airbuses and rocket ships – suggest, in this context, the collision of different cultural traditions and collective identities. However, if encounters with the unfamiliar were the *raison d'être* of Méliès's voyage films, the nature of the differences depicted changed over the years. Whereas the 1902 *Lune* showed a completely imaginary 'other', subsequent voyage films (made both by Georges Méliès and by his brother Gaston, whose work for the American branch of Star-Film will be discussed briefly at the end of this chapter) depicted more down-to-earth – if still somewhat fanciful or stereotypical – encounters with difference, reflecting a changing international climate.

Le Voyage dans la lune/A Trip to the Moon (1902)

Made in 1902, *Le Voyage dans la lune* was the film that first brought Méliès international fame – and it is the film that, even today, is the most widely recognized of Méliès's works. At first, however, he had difficulty persuading fairground exhibitors to buy it because of the high price resulting from the film's lavish production costs; so he lent the film to exhibitors free of charge for a single showing, confident that its popularity with audiences would convince exhibitors that they would recoup his asking price (560 FF for the black and white version, 1,000 FF for the hand-coloured version). Méliès's faith in the film paid off – at least in getting it widely distributed. By the same token, as we have seen, its widespread popularity prompted unscrupulous distributors, particularly in the United States, to make unauthorized copies of it, drastically reducing the profits that reverted to Méliès's production company. It was thus one of his most fantastical films, set on the moon, that brought Méliès crashing down to the harsh reality of international competition.

Le Voyage dans la lune was not only the first science fiction film, but also the first cinematic spoof of the genre. The moon had been a locus of narrative mystery and desire at least since the publication of Cyrano de Bergerac's *L'Autre Monde* in the seventeenth century. *Le Voyage dans la lune*, like *Le Voyage à travers l'impossible/The Impossible Voyage* (1904), was based in part on a fantasy stage play adapted by Adolphe Dennery from Jules Verne; Méliès at once revels in and lampoons the scientific exploits envisioned by Verne in *De la terre à la lune*, and by H. G. Wells in *Les premiers hommes dans la lune* (Sadoul 1970: 44). In its depiction of the exploration of a faraway place and hostile encounter with alien life forms, *Le Voyage dans la lune* can easily be read as a parable of colonial conflict. When the film was made, France was the second largest colonial power in the world, having emerged from a period of unprecedented imperial expansion at the end of the nineteenth century. While Méliès mocks the pretensions of colonialist accounts of the conquest of one culture by another, his film also thematizes social differentiation on the home front, as the hierarchical patterns on the moon are shown to bear a curious resemblance to those on earth.

The film opens on a congress of scientists dressed in flowing robes, long white wigs and pointed wizard caps, many of whom are arranged in bleacher-like rows that anticipate the stalls of onlookers in *Le Sacre d'Edouard VII/The Coronation of King Edward VII*, made later that year. On the left are a blackboard and lectern, below which sit three wizards, presumably in a secretarial capacity, who appear to be women dressed as men. Six more scientists enter from the right foreground, to mutual greetings, followed by six pages (women dressed in tightly fitting breeches) carrying telescopes like rifles in a military parade. The pages ceremoniously hand the telescopes to the scientists and exit. The bearded head wizard Barbenfouillis, played by Méliès, then enters to reverential acclaim; the six scientists hold up their telescopes which are transformed, through substitution splicing, into stools upon which they sit. Barbenfouillis lectures the group and draws a diagram on a blackboard of a rocket's trajectory, which provokes uproar among the scientists. Much excitement ensues, and Barbenfouillis throws wads of paper at his sceptical colleagues. He begins to stomp off, apparently threatening to abandon the trip, and is coaxed back by the others, who seem to have thrown their support behind the project. The men begin taking off their robes decorated with stars and planets, and change into dandyesque outfits of knee-breeches, long topcoats, top hats, and umbrellas. The costumes, especially in this first scene, heighten the effect of the absurd. The scientists' pointed hats connote a dubious wisdom made to seem all the more silly by their resemblance to dunce caps, recalling sketches for the clownish, eponymous hero of Jarry's *Ubu roi*, whose première in Paris Méliès had enthusiastically attended six years earlier (Malthête-Méliès 1973: 190). The scientists in the upper row wear enormous collars suggestive alternatively of Renaissance costumes or Gilles-like clown suits. Similarly, the dainty gentleman's costumes the explorers change into trivialize their undertaking, as though they were embarking upon a friendly game of billiards rather than a trip across the galaxy.

As the newly outfitted scientific explorers file off to the right, the scene dissolves to a workshop where builders hammer away at the spacecraft, which is shown in profile. The workshop bears a close resemblance to Méliès's film studio, with its greenhouse-like glass ceiling visible in the background. The explorers enter and express their delight at the sight of the partially-constructed rocket, congratulating the workers and climbing in to examine the interior. As they climb out again, one of them loses his balance and is scooped up by the others, providing a taste of slapstick that foreshadows the misadventures to come, and diminishing the dignity and impression of competence of the scientists by compar-ison with the capable, industrious workers. The scene dissolves to the next tableau, a rooftop view of an urban landscape replete with factories belching real smoke. The explorers enter from the right and crowd onto a balcony, pointing and gesturing toward the sky in the distance; one of them, in the foreground, peers through a telescope.

There is then another dissolve to the rocket's launch site on a wooden platform situated atop the town's tiled rooftops, whose pointed tips occupy the bottom quarter of the frame. On the wooden platform, which occupies the central and upper-left portion of the frame, a row of women dressed in tiny sailor suits stand at attention; a giant cylinder is situated in profile in the right third of the frame. The explorers climb up onto the platform, greet those present and gather in front of the cylinder, appearing to stand directly on the rooftops, from where they look down and tip their hats to unseen crowds below. (The lack of proportion here prefigures the moment in *Le Tunnel sous la Manche/Tunnelling the English Channel* (1907) when the French and British rulers tower above the English Channel.) The rocket appears from the left and the gentlemen climb in clumsily. A line of female sailors push the rocket into the cylinder before waving their hats triumphantly in the air while facing the camera – perhaps they are waving to more unseen crowds, as the explorers did a moment earlier, or perhaps they are breaking the diegesis by gesturing to the film's audience, in a self-conscious moment of cinematic attraction. The costumes worn by the female sailors evoke the centuries-long tradition of nautical exploration, now replaced by other means (land-based and flying vehicles), and by other destinations (space). As eroticized and trivialized caricatures of explorers, the female sailors both compensate for and remind us of the absence of women from the expedition: they are dressed to travel, but they go nowhere.

The scene then dissolves to a different view of the launch site, shown in a different set not in profile any longer but now from behind, as if the camera had swivelled forty-five degrees. This change of viewpoint provides a level of sophistication not often associated with Méliès by film historians eager to dismiss his work as primitive, and recalls a similar transition in *Le Royaume des fées/The Kingdom of the Fairies* (1903): as the ship lands on the sea bed, large bubbles rise through the water; then, there is a dissolve to a three-quarter view of the wrecked ship seen much closer up, now a part of the painted set.

In *Lune*, three sailors march forward ceremoniously and blow a trumpet, while a man in a white costume and broad-rimmed hat climbs a ladder to the left of the frame and lights the cannon's fuse. There is a flash and a puff of smoke at the end of the cylinder, and several townspeople rush in from the foreground, backs to the camera, to see off the rocket. This scene provides another example of Méliès's use of staging in depth, by showing movement along the camera axis, as in the *Attentat contre maître Labori* film in the *Affaire Dreyfus* series, and the town square scene in *Le Tunnel sous la Manche*. A dissolve then takes us to a shot of the moon in a painted sky framed by clouds. The moon grows larger, as if viewed from the approaching rocket: Hammond refers to this as a tracking shot (1974: 103), but Frazer points out (1979: 96) that this is the same technique Méliès used in *L'Homme à la tête de caoutchouc/Man with the Rubber Head*, made earlier the same year, in which the object being viewed was itself rolled on a ramp toward a stationary camera (what Abel calls 'the illusion of a dolly shot' (1998: 63)). This illusion of camera movement recalls the impression of a swivel shot created two scenes earlier through *mise en scène*.

As the moon approaches, its surface becomes more visibly anthropomorphic. A substitution splice shows the rocket landing in the moon's right eye at the left of the frame; the moon sticks its tongue out from the shock as part of its face melts frosting-like into its mouth. This is the film's most famous image, suggesting a literal shift in perspective that locates a gazing subject outside of Earth (a perspective that will be reinforced in the next scene, when the explorers glimpse the Earth from their location on the moon). This Copernican revolution in visual perception is aided by the logic of the film's narrative, which, as the explorers are shown on the moon for most of the rest of the film, has situated them within its eye, where the rocket has landed. Therefore, when they see the Earth, they see it quite literally from the moon's point of view, thus prefiguring the shot/reverse-shot structure that would become common currency in modern film-making.

Nonetheless, this film's complexity has often been under-played. One critic has written: 'C'était le cinéma primitif. Le langage cinématographique en était aux balbutiements; la caméra demeurait obstinément immobile; le montage restait encore à découvrir; on ignorait les ellipses (spatiale ou temporelle) et les débats psychologiques. L'attention du spectateur n'était pas canali-sée par un effet de caméra et l'oeil s'égarait dans le désordre foisonnant de l'image.'[1] While it is indeed true that Méliès's camera remained immobile, there is ample evidence, as we have seen, of both montage and ellipses; as for 'débats psychologiques', Barbenfouillis's petulant behaviour and megalomaniacal motives for conducting the expedition perhaps go some way toward satisfying this criterion of cinematic complexity.

The next scene appears by way of a cut, as the rocket is shown in profile landing on the moon's rugged terrain, seen close up. (This is effectively the second time we see the rocket land, from a different point of view. This modern editing technique, in which a single action is broken up in multiple shots, would be repeated in other Méliès films, such as *A la conquête du Pôle*, in which the

---

1 'This was primitive cinema. The language of film was still at the babbling stage; the camera remained obstinately immobile; editing had not yet been discovered; there was no knowledge of ellipses, either spatial or temporal, or psychological conflict. The spectator's attention was not guided by the camera, and the eye wandered across the teeming disorder of the image' (D'Hugues *et al.* 1986: 43).

airplane is shown landing on the pole in two consecutive shots from different vantage points.) The hatch opens and the explorers straggle out of the vessel (which conveniently disappears by means of substitution splicing) and gather in the right foreground to watch the earth rise in the background, as a piece of the set depicting jagged rock formations sinks out of sight – anticipating by well over half a century the famous photos of Earth taken from the moon.

After several adventures, the explorers are captured by a group of acrobatic crustaceans (the Selenites) and taken to their leader. The leader, whose features are particularly crustacean, sits on his throne at the left, flanked by female attendants and by six trident-bearing guards who stand in a row beside him, suggesting a parallel with the opening scene depicting the scientific congress with its six telescope-bearing pages. The explorers manage to escape, although not without a fight, and leap into their waiting rocket ship in the nick of time. We see the animated rocket splashing into a real ocean, using footage Méliès shot one summer while vacationing with his family in Normandy.

The next scene, set below the sea and shot through a real fish tank (a technique Méliès also used in *Le Royaume des fées* and *Visite sous-marine du Maine*), shows the vessel descending to the sea floor and then floating up to the surface and out of the frame. A dissolve brings us to the last scene of the American print, an animation in which the rocket is towed across the frame to shore by a sailing ship. The film's final scene shows the explorers' triumphant return to a celebratory reception in the town square, where a captured Selenite is paraded on a leash before the townspeople. The explorers link hands and dance around a statue of Barbenfouillis stomping on a shrunken moon as if it were a soccer ball.

Of course, both the pomposity of the scientific congress with which the film begins, and the triumphant return with which it concludes, are undermined by the explorers' hasty retreat from their encounter with the Selenites. But the themes of difference and conflict are not confined to the relationship between Earthlings and moon-dwellers. Subtending this film is a satire of social hierarchy: the interplanetary explorers' stint at the Selenites' court mirrors the hierarchical structure depicted at the scientific congress, as Barbenfouillis presides over his scientific disciples, the power conferred upon him by his intellectual prowess as arbitrary and absurd as that invoked by the crustacean king. *Le Voyage dans la lune* ultimately shows that, rather than being safely out of this world, the differences encountered by the intrepid explorers were very close to home. The structures of authority and class-based difference hinted at in *Le Voyage dans la lune* would be depicted more emphatically two years later in *Le Voyage à travers l'impossible/The Impossible Voyage* (1904), which brings class divisions to the fore.

Voyage à travers l'Impossible/The Impossible Voyage (1904)

This film has many features in common with Méliès's other voyage films, most notably *Le Voyage dans la lune*, on both a narrative and a stylistic level. The film opens on a crowded assembly of men and women in formal, *belle époque* dress. A man with a long black beard unfurls a drawing of fantastical vehicles, including a train heading off the top of a mountain (thus prefiguring one of the adventures depicted later in the film). The guests nod and smile approvingly. We then see the interior of a factory where the vehicle is being constructed, which, although structurally reminiscent of *Lune*, is actually closer to the 1912 *Conquête du Pôle*, because the assembly-line is mechanized. A servant – a woman dressed as a boy – attempts to serve the inventor tea; he responds by kicking the tray out of her/his hands. A party of visitors enters the factory, and are shown the vehicle they will be using for their journey – a cross between a dirigible and a submarine – as well as an ice tank. The tour of the factory continues in the next scene, set in the furnace room, where there are explosions (of more than one kind). One of the would-be travellers, a heavy-set woman, becomes so excited by the commotion that a worker sprays water on her to cool her down; this upsets her even more, and she dumps a bucket of water on the worker.

The next scene is set in a train station. Signs, some in French, some in English, and others a cross between the two languages, read: Depart, Switzerland, Enregistrement, Bagages, Luggage. People rush to make the train; the woman dressed as the servant boy is jostled and bumped, but fights back. We see the train pull off in the background. In the next scene, a tiny model of the train crosses the frame in the distance; then, a slightly bigger model crosses a mountain bridge going in the opposite direction closer to the foreground, giving the impression that the train has serpentined its way down the mountain. We then see a profile of three of the train's compartments; its occupants are covered with snow and ice. A dissolve shows the train pulling into a Swiss village; the passengers get off and pile into a streetcar. In the next scene, townspeople scatter as the streetcar crashes into a building, recalling similar scenes in *Le Raid Paris-Monte Carlo en deux heures/An Adventurous Automobile Trip*. Villagers are shown observing the scene from the foreground with their backs to the camera; this form of staging, though somewhat unusual for Méliès, is not unique in his *oeuvre*. It is another example of his occasional use of staging in depth.

We now see the interior of the building: the streetcar, much enlarged, steamrolls its way across a long table at which people are eating. Mayhem ensues. An animated version of the streetcar is then shown gliding over hill and dale, until it sails right off the side of a mountain. The next scene shows the streetcar crashing on the rocks below. Mountain climbers discover the injured passengers. A hospital scene then shows the travelling party to be unruly patients. Well again, the travellers pile onto a train shown almost head on. An animated version of the train makes its way up a mountain, continuing into the sky; the inventor's plans, indicated in the diagram shown in the first scene of the film, have been borne out. We are then treated to another one of Méliès's signature flights through the heavens, past shooting stars, planets, and meteor showers (represented by a lone sparkler). The following scene shows the anthropomorphic sun emerging from behind a cloud and approaching the camera (this is the same reverse-tracking technique used in *Lune*); as it approaches, the sun's face changes from a plaster mould to that of a man. When the sun yawns, the train flies into his mouth; he grimaces and spits out pieces of the train, belching smoke and sparks.

In the next scene, the train is shown crashing onto the sun's surface from above. This two-scene sequence replicates the rocket's landing in *Lune*. The travellers struggle out of the wreckage onto a hellish landscape complete with real fire. Feeling the heat, they wheel in the ice wagon thoughtfully provided for them by the inventor, and pile in. When the inventor opens the door a moment later, they are frozen in blocks of ice, so he lights a fire beneath the wagon, which thaws out the passengers. They then climb into the dirigible-submarine.

The next four linked scenes replicate the sequence from *Lune*. The vehicle glides off a cliff, and is then shown falling through the sky with a parachute attached. In the next shot, the capsule is shown landing in the ocean; here animation was combined with actual footage of the ocean. Underwater, we see the capsule gliding through the water, with white squiggly lines indicating ocean depths, and two real fish swimming in the foreground.

The following scene, however, is an imaginative addition to the *Lune* sequence. We see the travellers in the capsule under water using a telescope to look through a huge portal at the passing ocean scenery. An octopus rises up to the window and wriggles its legs; the passengers hastily close the portal. Explosions in the engine bring real fire and smoke, and the whole vehicle explodes.

At the seashore, sailors picnic beneath a lighthouse. An explosion knocks them backward. It should be noted that this is another example of two scenes showing the same occurrence from two different points of view, recalling the landing of the spacecraft in *Lune*, and the landing of the train on the sun earlier in this film. A piece of the capsule floats to the ground. The travellers emerge and are greeted warmly; they pull the young servant out of the portal, and s/he staggers and must be supported by the other travellers. After a big heroes' welcome in the town, we return to the setting of the first scene, where people bow respectfully as a group of old men enter with rolled-up scrolls and sit at a banquet table, suggesting that a similar adventure is about to begin.

Le Voyage à travers l'impossible juxtaposes the decadent sophis-tication of the upper classes with the no-nonsense 'simplicity' of their peasant or working-class counterparts. The jaded city folk, ill-adapted to the rigours of world (and celestial) travel, wreak havoc wherever they go, disrupting the lives of buccolic mountain climbers, alpine villagers, factory workers and sailors. They can-not even behave when wrapped up in bandages and confined to their beds in a hospital, insisting on making the nurses miserable. The hostile encounter between the heavy-set woman and the worker in the furnace room of the factory, as well as prefiguring the alternation between hot and cold that runs throughout the film (explosions/water; snow/meteor showers; melting heat/ice wagon; sun's surface/deep-sea diving), illustrates the tensions between the two social groups. The young servant who accom-panies the group on their trip is subjected to a litany of comic and not-so-comic catastrophes, including being kicked by the inventor as he tries to serve tea – an uncharacteristic moment of realistic violence that throws class divisions into stark relief (adding, since the servant is obviously played by a woman, a dimension of sexual violence, as discussed in the previous chapter).

In Méliès's next voyage film, the role of decadent trouble-maker will be played by a king; the next film reinforces the divisions between the elite and the popular outlined in *Le Voyage à travers l'impossible*. *Le Raid Paris-Monte Carlo en deux heures* (1905) goes further than any of Méliès's previous voyage films to thematize the emergence of the popular as a political force.

Le Raid Paris-Monte Carlo en deux heures/An Adventurous Automobile Trip (1905)

This film was based on a theatrical piece created by Méliès in col-laboration with Victor de Cottens for the Folies-Bergère the previous year. The film opens on a crowd scene. Police hold back excited spectators who have gathered in front of a painted set depicting the Paris Opéra-Garnier to watch King Leopold II of Belgium embark on his automobile race. The modern (for 1905) outfits worn by the onlookers suggest, somewhat unusually for a Méliès film, a contemporary setting. An extremely tall man, probably close to eight feet in height, towers above all the other spectators, enters into a shoving match with a policeman and then takes his place in the crowd. King Leopold pulls up, wearing a bulky fur coat; a man dressed in white stands in the passenger's seat. The king himself stands, and the pair greet well-wishers who pass in front of them, embracing them or shaking their hand. The extremely tall man rushes past the king, who holds up his fists in a joking manner and shakes his head in disbelief; then, a shorter-than-average man on skis walks by, greets the king, and lifts himself on the tips of the skis to kiss the tall man at the far right of the frame. The king waves goodbye to the cheering crowd and drives off toward the left.

In the American Star-Film catalogue, Méliès identifies the celebrities performing what may be the world's first film cameos, while simultaneously promoting the play from which the film sprang, and for whose success Méliès could take partial credit: 'the habitués of "Gay Paree" will recognize Mr. Notté, the celebrated singer of the Opera, Mr. Galipaux, one of the best French actors, Mme Jane Ivon, *The Giant Swede* in company with Little Tich, finally Mr. de Cottens, the author of the play then running at the Folies-Bergère – the latter is much beloved by Parisian theatre-goers' (BiFi Fonds Méliès GM011, unpaginated; original emphasis).

The same catalogue situates the scene described above after the following scene, which depicts a street with storefronts and passers-by going about their business; a man appears to be pestering women who pass. (Frazer's description of this film, based on a different version, has this scene first, following the scene in front of the Opéra.) The king's car enters the frame from the right, suggesting continuity of direction, and stops to the left of the shop in the foreground. After refuelling, the car reverses and runs over a police officer; a crowd gathers round as the car moves forward to reveal the man's flattened body. Men bring air pumps and attach them to the lifeless policeman (a life-size doll), whose pancake-thin body jumps at each burst of air. The crowd gathers round again; when it parts, the doll has been replaced by an actor who squirms and writhes histrionically at each pump. The crowd gathers round the man a third time, and there is an explosion, which sends one woman running diagonally toward the camera and out of the frame in the right foreground; the others drop to the ground and wriggle their legs in the air, as if reeling from the shock.

The following scene shows the car ploughing into a postman, and then dissolves to a model shot of a mountainous cartoon landscape with a miniature cut-out car gliding over hill and dale: the scenery moves from left to right while the car moves from right to left, giving the impression of a tracking shot. The car leaps over a precipice; as it flies through the air, there is a cut to the mountaintop on which it lands. It continues its course, only to fall straight off the side of a cliff. Another dissolve shows two guards pacing in front of a gate beside a sign that says 'Détour de Dijon'. A portly guard enters (Méliès in a heavily padded costume) and scolds the men for making fun of a plump passer-by, bucking them with his enormous stomach. The king's car enters from the right and the guard, with a little help from his stomach, manages to keep the car from going through the gate, pushing it back out of frame (recalling the suffragette in *A la conquête du Pôle* who shoves a man with her stomach); several more guards enter from the left foreground and meet the car as it makes another attempt. Together they push the car back out of frame once again. The car then enters a third time with several guards pulling it back from behind; it pushes up against the corpulent guard, who explodes. The car proceeds through the gates as guards fall back and townspeople run up to watch.

The scene then dissolves to a country market where young women in alpine dress (a geographical inaccuracy) tend stalls as a bourgeois couple examine their wares. Suddenly, startled, the couple look to the right, throw up their hands in fear, and run off to the left as a man, covered with rubble, comes hurtling into the frame as if propelled by an explosion, followed immediately by the king's car, which overturns the market stalls in its wake. Subsequent scenes show the car crashing into a building and driving over the roof of a blacksmith's shop.

The scene then cuts to an outdoor pavillion in three-quarter profile. As the townspeople settle into their seats on the grandstand, a couple of women enter and begin folk dancing for them on the grassy area below (this scene, like the triumphant homecoming in *Le Royaume des fées*, appears to have been shot outdoors). A gendarme rushes into the frame and shoos the women out of the way, just before the king's car rolls across the grass and up the ramp onto the grandstand, causing it to collapse before rolling off again toward the camera and slightly to the left of the frame. In the final scene, the car crashes into a truck, which disappears in a puff of smoke, causing a bystander to backflip toward the camera.

There can be no doubt that Méliès used his voyage films to satirize prevailing attitudes or individual personalities; as scientific pomposity was sent up in *Le Voyage dans la lune* and *La conquête du Pôle*, so King Leopold II's reputation for wreckless driving was skewered in *Le Raid Paris-Monte Carlo en deux heures*. In this film, however, the function of the king seems to transcend his individual foibles: when the monarchy butts up against *le peuple*, mayhem ensues. Villagers, shopkeepers, farmers, artisans, cheering crowds in both town and country – the king ploughs through them all, intrusive, disruptive, and entirely out of place. Part of the humour of these encounters derives from the confrontation between 'high' and popular culture: it is doubtless no accident that the king begins his journey in front of the Paris Opéra, at once a shrine to the lofty cultural pursuits of opera and ballet, and a symbol of Méliès's apocryphal discovery of stop-motion, a trick that would enhance film's popular appeal. The presence, too, in this scene, of the very tall and short actors evokes the circus and vaudeville, entertainment forms that were being threatened by the emergence of film as the popular medium that was fast becoming the form of entertainment accessible to the most people. The new leisure pursuits of automobile ownership and tourism, though the privileged domain of the wealthy, did not come with class-based cultural associations; they had popular appeal, and would become increasingly democratized throughout the century. As the king's car wreaks havoc wherever it goes, it appears out of place, as if to suggest the unsuitability of *ancien régime* political formations in a world witnessing the emergence of the popular as a cultural and political force. It is useful to recall in this context that the very first French film, the Lumières' *La Sortie d'usine*, marked not only the transition between two kinds of space, from the factory to the outside world, but also, and perhaps more important, a shift from work to leisure time, which would come to be filled increasingly by the new medium of film.

Although Méliès was clearly poking fun at a particular individual in *Le Raid Paris-Monte Carlo*, he came increasingly to exploit national stereotypes as the decade wore on. In his next two voyage films, as we shall see, it is the British who are taken for a ride.

Les Quat'cents farces du diable/The Merry Frolics of Satan (1906)

The obsession with speed that Méliès lampooned in *Le Raid Paris-Monte Carlo* resurfaced the next year in *Les Quat'cents Farces du diable*, which shows the trend toward increasing efficiency carried to a logical extreme. This film, one of Méliès's masterpieces, was shot in two different stages. The celestial voyage scenes had been filmed six months earlier than the rest, for inclusion in a multimedia stage production at the Châtelet theatre. Pleased with the results, Méliès decided to create a film into which he could slot the phantom coach ride.

When the film opens, the inventor William Crackford, dressed in tartan trousers, floor-length tartan coat, and pith helmet (apparently meant to represent the British national costume), is persuaded to follow an envoy to the alchemist Alcofribas's laboratory, complete with giant telescopes, bunsen burners, and a large, bat-like creature suspended from the ceiling. Crackford and his assistant John are subjected to a variety of theatrical torments, including chairs that grow taller and giant props that kick them or fall over on them. Alcofribas enters, followed by a group of smaller wizards, and offers Crackford a bunch of magical baseball-sized pills. He throws one on the ground, and a woman appears in a puff of smoke wearing diaphanous garments, before turning into an ogre (played by what appears to be a child wearing a giant ogre mask). The wizard refuses Crackford's attempts to pay him for the magic pills, instead making him sign a contract before leaving. Alcofribas reveals the smaller wizards to be women dressed – unusually – as women (though one is dressed as a man in renaissance costume): they are the Seven Deadly Sins. The wizard's costume falls off to reveal that he is actually ... Mephistopheles!

The next scene shows a Victorian bourgeois interior, where five women sit at a table. Crackford enters and drops a pill on the ground, where it becomes a trunk out of which leap two men in eighteenth-century costume. They pull another trunk out of the first one, and two shorter men in identical costume leap out. The same trick is repeated until there are five trunks and ten men, who start collapsing furniture and stuffing it in the trunks (as in *Le Locataire diabolique/The Diabolic Tenant* (1909)), which are lined up in a row. Each of the five women is lifted into a trunk, with Crackford placed in the trunk at the front of the line. The attendants prance around merrily for a moment, then make the trunks fall open to reveal a miniature train, each carriage containing a hunched-over woman, led by Crackford, with John above the engine (as well as a sled dragged along at the end with a woman clutching onto it). The train pulls away to the left, smoke billowing from its smokestack; Mephistopheles rises from a trap door in the floor, the eighteenth-century attendants bow humbly to their master, and are transformed into goblins. Satan disappears through his trap door and the goblins somersault away, disappearing in a puff of smoke.

In the next scene, the bridge over which the train is passing breaks in the middle, and some of the passenger carriages are plunged into the gorge below. A man climbs onto his roof in the foreground and observes the scene with his back to the camera; the first two carriages of the train, containing Crackford and John, pull away unscathed. The truncated train pulls in to a rustic village, and villagers fold up the carriages into trunks and carry them away. A chef appears on a balcony and ushers the travellers up to his inn, before turning into Mephistopheles, who sends two black-clad imps up into the inn. Inside, the two travellers are pursued frenetically by the imps; mayhem ensues, as the baddies appear and disappear from chutes and openings in the walls.

In the next scene, shot outdoors, the travellers jump onto a real coach with a real horse attached to it. The devil turns the horse into a nightmarish skeleton, and the coach into an ornate, hallucinatory vehicle before disappearing into thin air. A cook drives up in a real automobile (perhaps the only such appearance in a Méliès film). The devil reappears, shoves the cook out of the driver's seat and takes the wheel, butting the car up against the carriage, and pushing it forward. The next scene, a model shot, shows the tiny carriage against the sky, pushed by the devil's car. It soon becomes apparent that they are driving up the side of a sputtering volcano; clouds part to reveal the carriage riding through the heavens. John examines a shooting star from close up, while Crackford munches on a crescent moon as if it were a slice of watermelon. They pass by a parade of celestial creatures, including old-man Saturn emerging angrily from the door in his planet (as in *Voyage dans la lune*) and flying women bearing stars, to whom Crackford throws kisses and pokes friskily with his umbrella. The carriage stops briefly to yield to a woman pasted onto a huge star; when she has floated past, the carriage resumes its course, passing under three large stars with big human faces peering out of them.

The carriage is then seen falling through the sky, followed by the spinning horse skeleton, John, and Crackford with his umbrella open to break his fall. The rolling-backdrop technique used here appears to be the same one used in the 1903 *Faust aux enfers/The Damnation of Faust*, as Mephistopheles and Faust hurtle into the pit of hell. The next shot completes the fall, with the two travellers crashing through the ceiling of Crackford's home. Just as they think it's all over, the devil appears, pointing angrily to his contract, and whisks the men away through a chute in the floor. The final scene, set in hell, continues the downward movement of the previous shot, as John and Crackford are lowered into the frame. A huge monster face appears, out of whose mouth roll imps and then women with tridents and vaguely

Arabic-looking veils on their faces. Crackford is thrown onto a spit and slowly rotated over a real fire.

In this lively film, modern efficiency is epitomized by the trunks that unfold, like Felix the Cat's bag of tricks, to become a passenger train. The fantastical merges with the ultra-modern when the automobile is used to get the magical carriage started. In 1906, automobiles were a recent technological innovation, the wave of the future, and thus nearly as fantastical as a magic carriage; this image provides another illustration of technology's role as the new magic. The contract that Satan brandishes, and which leads to Crackford's downfall, symbolizes the increasing primacy accorded to business relations in a changing world. Crackford's hallucinogenic voyage is conducted at the expense of his own family, who are stuffed into the tiny train and then abandoned in the wreckage in the forest.

The film's macabre ending, with William Crackford roasting on a spit, must have been particularly satisfying for the more Anglophobic viewers of Méliès's films. Strained Anglo-French relations were a theme that Méliès carried over into a film he made later the same year, which anticipated the completion of the Channel Tunnel – as well as the attendant problems that ensued – by some ninety years.

Le Tunnel sous la Manche, ou Le Cauchemar franco-anglais/ Tunnelling the English Channel (1907)

This film differs from Méliès's other voyage films: although *Le Tunnel sous la Manche* contains scenes of a voyage (which in fact provide the film's climax), it does not emphasize the voyage itself, but rather the preparations for the trip. In his discussion of *Le Tunnel sous la Manche* Frazer laments the film's 'general loss of energy' (1979: 183), but to my mind, this is one of Méliès's wittiest and most engaging films. As its subheading, 'cauchemar franco-anglais' (Anglo-French nightmare), suggests, it emphasizes tensions between the two imperial powers, in a striking combination of whimsy and conflict.

The film opens on a stage split in two by a white wall (rather than by a split screen, an option that was available at the time). On the left, the British king's bedroom is denoted by the *fleur-de-lys* motif on the stairs leading to the monarch's raised bed; on the right, two men, King Edward (played by the same washroom attendant who starred in *Le Sacre d'Edouard VII*) and the French President play cards in the latter's chamber (denoted with a helpful 'RF', for *république française*) before each man, clad in nightshirt and floppy nightcap, retires to bed on his own side. Because the *fleur-de-lys* is normally used to emblematize the French, rather than the British, monarchy, its use here to denote the British side collapses the distinction between modes of government, monarchy and republic, suggesting, as we shall see, that there are more important distinctions to be made.

In the next scene, the beginning of an extended dream sequence, a remarkable cartoon-like illustrated set shows a cross-section of the English channel, with layers of coloured soil and rock formations descending far below the surface of the shore. The rulers enter and stand on the seashore in the upper part of the frame as animated waves churn and ships, blimps and balloons float across sea and sky. The men, gigantic in proportion to the landscape, peer through binoculars and a telescope at each other, laugh, wave, and blow kisses. As they reach across the channel to shake hands, their rubbery arms stretch to several times their normal length to meet each other; each then retracts his sore arm and rubs it. (François Jost has noted the pun implied in the image of the long *manches*, or sleeves, extending across the *Manche*, or Channel.[2]) The rulers make swimming and then digging gestures. Each brings out a giant corkscrew, which he twists into the ground (it is perhaps worth noting here that Lynne Kirby reads this film as 'an unconscious homosexual fantasy in an overdetermined space of terror, the train tunnel' (Kirby 1997: 94). The men then exit and two workmen return in their place (it is possibly the rulers themselves in work clothes) and hack at the ground with picks. Two women wearing classically-draped robes enter carrying flags bearing the words 'Britannia' and 'RF', respectively.

2 'Le rêve de Méliès' in Malthête & Marie 1996: 242n.

The next three scenes show workers first on the English side, then on the (more technologically sophisticated) French side digging away. Each of the rulers pays a visit to the worksite of his respective country. Democracy and distinction cancel each other out comically in a filmographic description of the French President's visit: 'Le Président ... sort des décorations qu'il distribue à tout le monde, comme il en a trop, il en accroche même une au revers de l'habit de son valet'.[3] Finally, both sides share the screen as they complete the tunnel, to general rejoicing; in the water above, the fishes greet each other with kisses. Subsequent scenes show a model train travelling through the tunnel, and then a train station as the French presidential train (marked 'First Class') departs to much fanfare.

The following scene, shot outdoors, shows a town square. A parade of Salvation Army women marches in, followed by the French president, who is repeatedly approached by men trying to shine his shoes who are pulled away by the police. King Edward enters from the front left of the frame with his retinue, whose backs are facing the camera (in another example of in-depth staging); as the two leaders greet one another in the background, a man sweeping in the foreground and two men who attempt to shine the president's shoes are carried off by a policeman. An elaborately groomed French poodle crosses the frame; the two leaders walk arm-in-arm down and out of frame as a Frenchman (dressed in a Napoleon hat) and an Englishman (dressed in a riding costume) in the crowd embrace.

A bilingual intertitle with the words 'Le Réveil/Awaking!' (sic) then gives way to a shot of an animated tunnel, where two trains crash into each other. Black smoke fills the frame, then real water pours in from the top. A dissolve takes us back to the split stage depicting the rulers tucked up in bed, tossing and turning until their bed posters fall on top of them simultaneously. The French president runs through the dividing door to the English side; the

---

3 'The President ... takes out medals which he distributes to everyone, but as he has too many, he even pins one on the jacket of his valet'. (*Filmographie* (author unknown, but probably either Méliès himself or Georges Sadoul), BiFi Fonds Méliès, GM018.)

men shake hands and describe their dream to each other in frantic pantomime. A visitor is announced, and enters the president's room with rolled-up plans; when he unfurls his diagram, which bears the words, 'Tunnel sous la manche/Submarine tunnel', he is unceremoniously ejected.

Le Tunnel sous la Manche, in which human beings tower over a liliputian English Channel, offers a literal interpretation of the clichéd expression, 'It's a small world'. In the first years of the twentieth century, the globe was shrinking by the minute, as the multiplying circuits of travel, communications, and international finance linked increasing numbers of communities. The idea of building a tunnel to connect Britain and France was under discussion when Méliès made his fantastical film, and discussions continued until the construction of Channel Tunnel was finally completed in the 1990s. (Historical hindsight puts an amusing spin on Frazer's dismissive remark, written in 1979, that 'schemes for a tunnel between England and France are still seriously discussed' (183)).

Méliès's film abounds in, but also plays on, national stereotypes, from the sanctimoniousness of the Salvation Army to the preciosity of the elaborately groomed French poodle, and in the men who greet each other in the afterglow of the tunnel's initial success, each dressed in what is apparently supposed to be his national costume. The bilingual intertitle (one of the first uses of intertitles by Méliès) indicates the international profile of the market for his films. Méliès fans the flames of competition between Britain and France (who were, after all, keen imperial rivals, carving up large portions of Africa and Asia between them) by throwing little bones alternately to each of the two nations: first, Edward's bed is shown to be higher up off the ground than President Fallières's bed, hinting at a subtle superiority or domination of the former over the latter; but then, as the tunnel is being dug, the French side is shown to be much more hi-tech than the British side – even though Britain was more industrialized than France at the time. Once the tunnel is complete, however, the mechanized equipment is shown distributed evenly on both sides, suggesting the effectiveness of face-to-face contact as a democratizing force. It is worth noting that the levelling of national differences does not eradicate class-based inequalities, as the scene in which the police forcibly and repeatedly remove sweepers and shoe shiners from the rulers' sight illustrates. The possibility of an international brotherhood of man seems to be a privilege reserved for the ruling élite and the wealthy (such as the men in the Napoleon hat and riding costume): President Fallières rides in a train compartment marked 'First Class', further eroding the myth (not to mention the language) of republican *égalité*.

But all dreams must come to an end. The difficulty of passing between the two countries was demonstrated as early as the 1897 *Entre Calais et Douvres/Between Calais and Dover*, where a rough crossing was signalled by overturned deck furniture and a passenger's relentless vomiting. The giddy idealism that marks much of the 1907 film eventually comes crashing down, resulting in a rude awakening – or, as the intertitle has it, an 'awaking'. Like the little boy who is transformed into two fighting boys representing Britain and the US in Méliès's 1898 *Illusions fantasmagoriques/The Famous Box Trick*, the suggestion is that unity between France and Britain would also be short-lived. The spirit of cooperation in which *Le Tunnel sous la Manche* opens ends literally in nightmare, as the rulers of France and Britain, ever the cordial *bon-vivants*, agree to disagree.

A long haul: From *Le Voyage dans la lune* to *A la conquête du Pôle*

Both the continuity and the development of Méliès's work may be seen if we compare two films with similar themes made a decade apart. *Le Voyage dans la lune* (1902) and *A la conquête du Pôle* (1912) were both inspired by fantasy stage plays adapted by Adolphe Dennery from Jules Verne stories. Both tell a tale of explorers travelling to a distant land, where they must battle an alien force (the Selenites, the snow monster) before returning triumphantly. But the second film contains an international dimension that the earlier film did not, which reflects the changing times. It is the films' striking parallels that bring out their even more striking differences.

Both films open with a meeting of scientific explorers who are attempting to design a vehicle that will enable them to travel to an unexplored destination, and both contain an early scene depicting the construction of the vehicle. However, whereas in *Lune* the scene shows a carpenter's workshop with men hammering pieces of wood, *Conquête* shows, according to the preceding intertitle, 'L'usine électrique où le professeur Maboul a réalisé son oeuvre',[4] with an automated assembly line, reflecting the great advances in the industrial use of electricity and automation between 1902 and 1912. Similarly, sweeping advances were made in film techniques, one of these being the introduction of intertitles, which Méliès (or Zecca) uses in 1912 but not in 1902.

The most explicit difference between the two films, however, is apparent in the international dimension of the later film, which is not present in *Lune*. Frazer suggests that the international flavour of *Conquête* reflects the changing face of the film industry: 1912 was Méliès's last year of production, as he succumbed to largely international competition (Frazer 1979: 217). It is certainly also possible that the film's title is an ironic allusion to Pathé's slogan, 'A la conquête du monde'. However, the significance of *A la conquête du Pôle* extends beyond the film industry itself to reflect, on a global political scale, increasing international tensions on the eve of the First World War.

Whereas in *Lune* there is no depiction of national differentiation within the group of explorers (and indeed, no suggestion of national identity at all except for the French flag shown waving among the group of onlookers who gather to see the rocket off), in *Conquête*, the team of explorers is international: there is a Chinese mandarin, a Japanese samurai, an American cowboy, a Mexican mariachi, and what seems to be a caricature of a German – corpulent with a bushy beard and alpine walking stick. The team appear to be working in co-operation, but there is not enough room in the vehicle for everyone, and although alternative transport is arranged, one of the delegates, the Chinese man, manages to get left behind – along with the unfortunate exploding suffragette, who was never invited to join the team in the first place

4 'the electricity-powered factory where Professor Maboul made his creation'.

(the bilingual sign informing the woman that the aérobus is 'complet/full', motivated diegetically by the fact that Mrs. Pankhurst was English, and commercially perhaps by Méliès's dependence on the English-speaking market, adds to the film's international flavour). So, what begins as a collaborative effort becomes fragmented and competitive. The theme of international competition surfaces again in unmistakable terms when we are shown the collection of national flags planted around the Pole. The competitive atmosphere is also echoed in the film's title: the gentle-sounding 'voyage' of 1902 has, by 1912, become a 'conquête'.

Méliès had alluded to mounting international tensions as early as 1908, in a film that is now lost, *La Civilisation à travers les âges*. Sadoul describes the final scene thus: 'Au dénouement, à la Conférence de la Paix, les diplomates montaient à la tribune où figurait une banderole où était inscrit le mot PAX, en brandissant la pancarte: "ARBITRAGE, LIMITATION DES ARMEMENTS, FRATERNITÉ." On les applaudissait. Et sitôt après commençait une violente bagarre, conclusion et moralité de cette cavalcade à travers les siècles' (Sadoul 1970: 59).[5] Méliès's ironic humour does not conceal his pessimism.

Méliès's depictions of the changing face of international relations included not only images of imperial rivalries and assorted struggles for power in the political arena, but representations of other kinds of cultural encounters as well. Many of his films trade in exoticism (and indeed, in overt racism), which had special appeal to viewers at the height of the imperial era. At the turn of the century, all things exotic were in vogue, from *littérature coloniale* (Loti, Mille, Benoît) and theatre to home furnishings and painting (*chinoiserie*). The increased opportunities for travel afforded by developments in transportation technologies meant that far-flung groups of people were coming into contact with each other, causing tensions for those not accustomed to meeting people whose cultural practices differed from theirs.

5 'In the final scene, at the Peace Congress, the diplomats climbed onto the platform where there figured a banner inscribed with the word PAX, while they held up a sign reading 'ARBITRATION, DISARMAMENT, BROTHERHOOD'. The audience applauded. And at that moment a violent brawl erupted, conclusion and moral of this cavalcade through the centuries.'

Le Bourreau turc/The Terrible Turkish Executioner (1904) exploits the stereotype of Oriental despotism and cruelty. Although many of Méliès's films feature dismemberment and decapitation, the violence of such acts is minimized where there is no weapon, or where the dismemberment is self-inflicted; when Méliès pulls his own head off in *Le Mélomane* or *Un homme de tête/Four Trouble-some Heads* (1898), the impression is not of an act of violence, but instead of a magic disappearing act. In *Le Bourreau turc*, on the other hand, a sword is used to commit an act of violence, and the dismemberment of the victims appears as a graphic illustration of an uncivilized penal system. The heads lying on the ground are props, rather than the usual superimposed living specimens; they look as though they have weight and substance, which lends them a visceral immediacy closer to Tarantino's lurid (though ironic) gore than to Méliès's standard dancing Disney-style body parts.

Star-Film's English catalogue provides this synopsis of a film now lost, *L'Omnibus des toqués/Off to Bloomingdale Asylum* (1901):

> An omnibus arrives drawn by an extraordinary mechanical horse. On the top are four negroes. The horse kicks and upsets the negroes, who are changed into white clowns. They slap each others' faces and by the blows become black again. They kick each other and become white once more. Finally they are all merged into one large negro, and when he refuses to pay his carfare, the conductor sets fire to the omnibus and the negro bursts into a thousand pieces'.[6]

The fact that the omnibus passengers are African is apparently meant to reinforce the departure from normalcy connoted in the word *toqués*, a colloquialism meaning 'loonies'. The transform-ation of the black men into white clowns posits an equivalence between African identity and foolishness. Finally, the violence with which the film ends is legitimated as an act of retribution for a crime committed, as we have seen in the case of many of the depictions of women in Méliès's films. The image of several Africans 'merging into one large negro' illustrates graphically the exoticist impulse to lump individuals deemed different together

6 Cited in Sadoul 1947: 15.

into a stereotypical mass identity, a 'them' opposed to an equally arbitrary 'us'.

Another film that plays on transformations from black to white is *Salon de coiffure/In the Barber Shop* (1908). Frazer gives the following description:

> Inside the barber shop two customers are getting their hair done. A dandy with blond curls admires his coif and departs with a lady. Two new clients enter, a fat lady and a black man. Both take their places in the barber chairs, but not before the black man has goosed the woman and made lascivious approaches. A huge power-driven brush is applied to the frizzy wig. The distracted barber lets the brush slip over the face of his frenzied customer. When he emerges from this abuse the customer delightedly discovers that he has been brushed white. The woman in the other chair rises to discover that she has turned black. She angrily throws equipment around the shop and storms out in a passionate pursuit of the newly white customer. The barbers convulse with laughter, knocking over a box of talcum, which brings on a general sneezing fit (Frazer 1979: 195–6).

In the beginning of the film, the African customer's credentials of racial authenticity are established when he is shown exhibiting stereotypical sexual aggressiveness, thereby making the subsequent transformation all the more sensational. His delight upon turning white contrasts markedly with the anger of the white woman who has become black, opposing a 'fortunate' turn of events to an 'unfortunate' one, making it clear which situation is the more desirable. (Méliès's own synopsis of the film concludes: 'On imagine la joie de celui qui est devenu blanc et la rage de la dame'.)[7] Another lost film made the same year, *New-York Paris en Automobile/Mishaps of the N.Y.–Paris Race* (1908), includes a scene of retribution that recalls that from *L'Omnibus des toqués*: 'La Cuisine automobile. – Enfin, à la dernière auto, est attelée une cuisine portative. Le Chef est déjà occupé à préparer le déjeuner, lorsqu'un nègre survient et veut goûter à la sauce; furieux, le cuisinier lui retourne le contenu d'une casserole sur la tête, à la

---

7 'You can imagine the joy of the newly whitened person and the rage of the woman'.

grande joie des spectateurs' (Cited in Bessy & Lo Duca 1961: 99).[8] Here, the very presence of an African is represented as one more 'mishap', a nuisance to be repelled, and becomes the butt of a humiliating practical joke enjoyed by those watching.

Le Cake-Walk infernal/The Infernal Cakewalk (1903) features African-American dancers with the addition of brown make-up applied to their faces performing the dance that swept Europe that year. The merriment takes place in hell, with even Mephisto-pholes (played, of course, by Méliès, agile as ever) being carried away by the excitement, to the point that his legs are separated from his body, flailing about rhythmically six inches or so from his torso, a trick that is then repeated with his arms. The film, one of Méliès's most euphoric creations, is of course sending up the popular dance craze, but it is also suggesting that the exotic is infectious: everyone who comes into contact with the dance is caught up in it, like the unfortunate explorers who are sucked onto the magnetic North Pole in *A la conquête du Pôle* . In *Le Cake-Walk infernal*, dozens of dancers crowd frenetically into the frame in a riotous finale, as if prey to a demonic possession. The film associ-ates exotic alterity with the fantastical other-worldliness connoted by the devil, as if the supernatural and the exotic were equally incomprehensible, and the inhabitants of each world equally improbable. Finally, in depicting the black couple as the centre-piece of the number, the film is cultivating the stereotypical link between Africans and dance, promoting a racial identity subsumed in corporeal agility and rhythm. Like Jean Epstein's 'corps noir' – the black body of the camera that is an extension of the mobile human body through which to view an even more mobile world – the black bodies that Méliès displays are objects to look into and through, to see the 'unknown' world that audiences always know they will find (Epstein, 'The Cinema Continues', in Abel 1988: 64). The black body accords viewers gratification by serving as a lens through which their desires are projected.

8 'Lastly, in the rear wagon, there is a makeshift kitchen. The Chef is already busy preparing the midday meal, when a negro appears and tries to taste the sauce; furious, the cook dumps the contents of a saucepan on his head, to the great delight of the spectators.'

The projection of exoticist desires is very apparent in the film career of Méliès's brother Gaston, who, after setting up the American Wildwest Company and producing films (mostly Westerns) in New Jersey, Texas and California from 1909 to 1912, embarked upon a tour of the South Pacific to film adventure movies. Gaston's letters to his son Paul, who was managing the New York office of Star-Film, reveal the incongruity between prevailing preconceptions about native savagery and reality. On 21 August 1912, Gaston wrote from Tahiti: 'L'île de Tahiti a deux inconvénients: 1 – il n'y a rien de confortable comme hôtels et 2 – les indigènes sont déjà trop civilisés pour pouvoir servir facilement dans les vues.'[9] The irony of Gaston's somewhat incompatible desires (for both modern hotels and inhabitants untouched by civilisation) seems to be unintended. What matters for his exotic films is not capturing a sense of the surroundings as they appear, but instead, creating the illusion of nature by means of artifice. This contradiction is reinforced in a letter Gaston wrote from Sydney, Australia on 31 October of the same year (presumably referring to shooting done earlier in New Zealand): 'On ne trouve plus de Maoris hommes tatoués, il n'y a que les femmes qui se fassent encore tatouer au menton. Dans la vue 97, il y a trois scènes qu'on a dû refaire parce que les naturels avaient oublié de se tatouer avec du fard' (61).[10] The use of the word 'naturel' instead of the more common 'indigène' (or 'natif') underscores the paradox of a nature that is not natural enough, and must be made up to look more natural – more 'different', in other words, from the intended viewers.

The value placed on exoticism indicates a desire to preserve cultural differences that were threatened with disappearance as contact between cultures increased. The specific details of the difference mattered less than the general impression of, as it were, undifferentiated difference. Hence the hodgepodge of exoticist

9 'The island of Tahiti has two disadvantages: 1) there are no comfortable hotels and 2) the natives are already too civilised to be useful in filming' (Malthête (ed.) 1988: 23).

10 'There are no more male Maoris with tattoos to be found; only the women still tattoo their chins. In film 97, there are three scenes that we had to redo because the natives had forgotten to draw tattoos on with makeup.'

signifiers present in a (Georges) Méliès film such as *L'Oracle de Delphes/The Oracle of Delphi* (1903), which is replete with Egyptian decor, or *Le Palais des mille et une nuits/The Palace of the Arabian Nights* (1905), which shows what the American Star-Film catalogue describes as a 'rajah' performing 'Buddhist rites' involving the sacrifice of 'vestal virgins' at the 'Temple of Siva'. Tableau 19, 'The Miraculous Caves', boasts an '[e]xact reproduction of the celebrated "Elephantine Cave" in British India', though the costumes and sets evoke a middle-Eastern, rather than an Indian, setting (BiFi Fonds Méliès GM011). As early as 1900, Méliès's catalogue listed a short film, to be inserted at the end of a programme, entitled *Vue de remerciements au public/Thanking the Audience*, which consisted of several characters, one by one, displaying the phrase 'Thank you, come again' in several languages (Malthête 1996a: 123).

The increasing awareness of the international community displayed in Méliès's work coincided with the end of an era – the end of the *belle époque*, the end of both Georges and Gaston's film careers – and the beginning of a time in which local particularities were forced to confront other local particularities as the planet shrank due to developing networks of communication and transportation. Many aspects of culture (the film industry, politics, war) were being reconfigured on a global scale, and art was becoming increasingly commodified, valued for its capacity to be mechanically reproduced and disseminated. It is the greatest irony that Méliès, whose artisanal style could not compete with the new practices of mass production, was condemned by the very industry he helped create, and that he was brought down in the end by the fulfilment of Star-Film's motto: 'Le monde à la portée de la main'.[11]

References

Abel, R. (1988), *French Film Theory and Criticism 1907-1939*, vols I & II, Princeton, NJ, Princeton University Press.

11 'The world at your fingertips'.

—— (1998), *The Ciné Goes to Town*, Berkeley, CA, University of California Press.

Bessy, M. and Duca, L. (1961), *Georges Méliès, Mage*, Paris, Pauvert.

D'Hugues, P. *et al.* (eds) (1986), *Le Cinéma français: le muet*, Paris, Atlas.

Frazer, J. (1979), *Artificially Arranged Scenes*, Boston, G. K. Hall and Company.

Hammond, P. (1974), *Marvellous Méliès*, London, Gordon Fraser.

Kirby, L. (1977), *Parallel Tracks: The Railroad and Silent Cinema*, Exeter, University of Exeter Press.

Malthête, J. (1996a), 'Méliès et le conférencier', *Iris* 22, Autumn.

Malthête, J. (ed.) (1988), Gaston Méliès: *Le Voyage autour du monde de la G. Méliès Manufacturing Company*, Paris, Association 'Les Amis de Georges Méliès'.

Malthête, J. and Marie, M. (eds.) (1997), *Georges Méliès l'illusionniste fin de siècle?* Paris, Presses de la Sorbonne Nouvelle.

Malthête-Méliès, M. (1973), *Méliès l'Enchanteur*, Paris, Hachette

Conclusion

This study has sought to re-evaluate Méliès's place in film history by examining some of the myths surrounding his work. These myths have been all-pervasive, leading many film students and scholars to accept them unquestioningly. However, by acknowledging Méliès's status as an *auteur* working independently to make a distinctive mark on the films he wrote, designed, directed, edited, produced and starred in, it is possible to replace these myths with a more accurate assessment of Méliès's legacy.

Myth 1: Méliès made primarily fairy tales and fantasies, characterised by their childlike naiveté

As we have seen, Méliès worked within a wide range of genres, which included newsreels, *actualités reconstituées*, magic acts, political satire, commercial advertisements, erotic or 'stag' films, historical epics, melodramas, science fiction, and, with the help of his brother Gaston, Westerns and action-adventures. The extent of this variety belies the exclusive association of Méliès with fantasy, and the sharp-edged wit that characterizes most of his films certainly undermines any impression of naive innocence devoid of worldly concerns. Many of Méliès's films overtly or implicitly problematize the relation between fantasy and realism and, by extension, film's relation to the worlds it depicts.

Myth 2: Méliès's style is exclusively theatrical, with little or nothing in the way of specifically cinematic features or effects.

Méliès did not merely produce 'filmed theatre', but used a number of cinematic techniques such as close-ups, multiple exposure and continuity editing. The special effects that he developed were often innovative and always sophisticated, requiring elaborate preparation. As Jacques Malthête has shown, the so-called 'arrêt de caméra' technique always involved careful splicing or 'collage'; similarly, effects such as transparencies, replication and super-imposition entailed precise positioning at both the profilmic and post-production stages of the multiple-exposure process.

Additionally, Méliès sometimes used deep staging, with charac-ters moving back and forth along the camera axis, and he created the illusion of camera movement through the use of moving backdrops and matte shots of objects approaching the camera.

Myth 3: Méliès's work is largely devoid of narrative structure, and is consequently qualitatively different from that of most film-makers who followed him. His films may not, therefore, be analyzed using the tools of modern film theory.

I hope to have shown that Méliès's films lend themselves to narrative analysis. Although I have used a model of structuralist analysis as an example, the implication is that Méliès's work can be examined using a variety of approaches. Even Méliès's shortest films, while undeniably full of exhibitionist spectacle, also contain a strong narrative component. As in other films, attractions and narration interact to form a complex and internally heterogeneous semiotic universe. Méliès's films can and should be analyzed as cinematic texts with thematic and symbolic coherence, both individually and in intertextual relation to one another. As texts, they at once reflect and engage with preoccupations of the historical context in which they were produced. In particular, prevailing anxieties about sexual and cultural difference were magnified at a time when the women's suffragist movement was gaining momentum, and when patterns of immigration and the threat of war made the world a much smaller place.

What is most clear is that Méliès was a Janus-faced figure linking two centuries: he drew upon and developed the theatrical traditions of the nineteenth, but he also had a profound influence on cinematic art of the twentieth. It is only by acknowledging the depth and diversity of Méliès's contribution to film history that we may stop relegating it to the status of 'primitive otherness' and recognize its kinship with the work of later film-makers, as well as its suitability for analysis using techniques of structuralist, post-structuralist, and post-post-structuralist film theory. It should no longer be necessary to argue, as Pierre Jenn did so eloquently in 1984, that Méliès was indeed a 'cinéaste', or film-maker in the sense in which it is understood today, rather than an uncinematic precursor of modern film-makers (Jenn 1984). He was an *auteur* in every sense, and his work paved the way for future *auteurs*.

Like the devil's legs shown dancing in the air several inches from his torso in *Le Cake-Walk infernal/The Infernal Cakewalk* (1903), Méliès's work has been detached from the body of film history. The traditional opposition between Méliès and Lumière has long been dismantled; it is now time to question the rigidity of the distinction between Méliès and the century of film-makers he has (so far) inspired.

References

Jenn, P. (1984), *Georges Méliès cinéaste*, Paris, Albatros.

Filmography

Approximately 170 of the 500 or so films Méliès made are known to have survived – only these are listed in this Filmography. Production dates and film lengths can vary according to the source or archive consulted. Determining the running time of films is not an exact science, because projection speeds for early film varied and continue to vary, but as a rough guide, it can be assumed that twenty metres of film corresponds to 50–60 seconds of running time. Méliès did not include credits in his films, so none are provided here. This information has been compiled and adapted from Malthête and Marie 1997; Abel 1998; Frazer 1979; and the Warwick Trading Company Catalogue. An asterisk (*) denotes a literal English translation where no known translation has been found. Several films made in 1908 were given English titles only.

1896

Une nuit terrible (*A Terrible Night*) no. 26; 20 m
Escamotage d'une dame chez Robert-Houdin (*The Vanishing Lady*), no. 70; 20 m
Le Manoir du diable (*The Haunted Castle*), nos 78–80; 60 m

1897

Combat naval en Grèce (*Naval Combat in Greece*), no. 110; 20 m
Entre Calais et Douvres (*Between Calais and Dover*), no. 112; 20 m
L'Auberge ensorcelée (*The Bewitched Inn*), nos. 122–3; 40 m
Après le bal (*After the Ball*), no. 128; 20 m

1898

Visite sous-marine du 'Maine' (*Divers at Work in the Wreck of the* Maine), no. 147; 20 m

Panorama pris d'un train en marche (*Panorama from the Top of a Moving Train*), no. 151; 20 m

Illusions fantasmagoriques (*The Famous Box Trick*), no. 155; 20 m

Guillaume Tell et le Clown (*Adventures of William Tell*), no. 159; 20 m

La Lune à un mètre (*The Astronomer's Dream*), nos 160–2; 60 m

Un homme de têtes (*The Four Troublesome Heads*), no. 167; 20 m

La Tentation de Saint-Antoine (*The Temptation of St Anthony*), no. 169; 20 m

1899

Salle à manger fantastique (*A Dinner under Difficulties*), no. 171; 20 m

L'Ours et la Sentinelle, no. 182; 20 m (listed in Malthête 1998 as an unconfirmed Méliès film)

L'Impressionniste fin de siècle (*An Up-to-Date Conjuror*), no. 183; 20 m

Le Diable au couvent (*The Devil in a Convent*), nos 185–7; 60 m

Le Portrait mystérieux (*A Mysterious Portrait*), no 196; 20 m

L'Affaire Dreyfus (*The Dreyfus Court-Martial*)

    La Dictée du bordereau (*Arrest of Dreyfus*), no. 206; 20 m

    L'Ile du Diable (*Dreyfus at Devil's Island – Within the Palisade*), no. 207; 20 m

    Mise aux fers de Dreyfus (*Dreyfus Put in Irons – Inside a Cell at Devil's Island*), no. 208, 20 m

    Suicide du colonel Henry (*Suicide of Colonel Henry*), no. 209; 20 m

    Débarquement à Quiberon (*Landing of Dreyfus from Devil's Island*), no. 210; 20 m

    Entretien de Dreyfus et de sa femme à Rennes (*Dreyfus in Prison of Rennes*), no. 211; 20 m

    Attentat contre Maître Labori (*The Attempt against Maître Labori*), no. 212; 20 m

    Bagarre entre journalistes (*The Fight of Journalists at the Lycée*), no. 213; 20 m

    Le Conseil de guerre en séance à Rennes (*The Court Martial at Rennes*), nos 214–15; 40 m

Cendrillon (*Cinderella*), no. 219-24; 120 m

Le Chevalier mystère (*The Mysterious Knight*), nos 226–7; 40 m

1900

Les Miracles du Brahmine (*The Miracles of Brahmin*), nos 237–40;
    80 m
La Vengeance du gâte-sauce (*The Cook's Revenge*), no. 243; 20 m
L'Homme-orchestre (*The One-Man Band*), nos 262–3; 40 m
Jeanne d'Arc (*Joan of Arc*), nos 264–75; 250 m
Le Livre magique (*The Magic Book*), nos 289–91; 60 m
Rêve de Noël (*The Christmas Dream*), nos 298–305; 160 m
Nouvelles Luttes extravagantes (*The Wrestling Sextette*), nos 309–10;
    70 m
Le Déshabillage impossible (*Going to Bed Under Difficulties*), nos 312–
    13; 40 m
Le Savant et le Chimpanzé (*The Doctor and the Monkey*), no. 317; 20 m

1901

La Chrysalide et le papillon (also *Le Brahmane et le Papillon*) (*The
    Brahmin and the Butterfly*), nos 332–3; 40 m
Dislocations mystérieuses (*Extraordinary Illusions*), nos 335–6; 35 m
Barbe-bleue (*Blue-beard*), nos 361–70; 210 m
L'Homme à la tête en caoutchouc (*The Man with the Rubber Head*), nos
    382–3; 50 m

1902

Le Sacre d'Edouard VII (*The Coronation of King Edward VII**)
    (uncatalogued)
L'Oeuf du sorcier (also: *L'Oeuf Magique Prolifique*) (*Prolific Magical
    Egg*), nos 392–3; 40 m
Voyage dans la lune (*A Trip to the Moon*), nos 399–411; 260 m
Les Trésors de Satan (*The Treasures of Satan*), nos 413–14; 50 m
L'Homme-Mouche (*The Human Fly*), nos 415–16; 40 m
La Femme volante (*Marvellous Suspension and Evolution*), nos 417–18;
    40 m
L'Équilibre impossible (*An Impossible Balancing Feat*), no. 419; 25 m
Chirurgie fin de siècle (also: *Une indigestion*) (*Up-to-Date Surgery*), nos
    422–5; 85 m
Le Voyage de Gulliver à Lilliput et chez les Géants (*Gulliver's Travels
    Among the Lilliputians and the Giants*), nos 426–9; 80 m
La Guirlande merveilleuse (*The Marvellous Wreath*), nos 445–8; 80 m

1903

Un malheur n'arrive jamais seul (*Misfortune Never Comes Alone*), nos 451–2; 50 m

Le Cake-Walk infernal (*The Infernal Cake Walk*), nos 453–7; 100 m

La Boîte à malice (*The Mysterious Box*), nos 458–9; 50 m

Le Puits fantastique (*The Enchanted Well*), nos 462–4; 70 m

L'Auberge du bon repos (*The Inn Where No Man Rests*), nos 465–9; 100 m

La Statue animée (*The Drawing Lesson*), nos 470–1; 50 m

La Flamme merveilleuse (*The Mystical Flame*), no. 472; 35 m

Le Sorcier (*The Witch's Revenge*), nos 473–5; 65 m

L'Oracle de Delphes (*The Oracle of Delphi*), no. 476; 30 m

Le Portrait spirite (*A Spiritualist Photographer*), nos 477–8; 40 m

Le Mélomane (*The Melomaniac*), nos 479–80; 50 m

Le Monstre (*The Monster*), nos 481–2; 50 m

Le Royaume des fées (*The Kingdom of the Fairies*), nos 483–98; 320 m

Le Chaudron infernal (*The Infernal Cauldron*), nos 499–500; 40 m

Le Revenant (*The Apparition*), nos 501–2; 50 m

Le Tonnerre de Jupiter (*Jupiter's Thunderbolts*), nos 503–5; 70 m

Le Parapluie fantastique (*Ten Ladies in One Umbrella*), nos 506–7; 55 m

Tom Tight et Dum-Dum (*Jack Jaggs and Dum Dum*), nos 508–9; 50 m

Bob Kick, l'enfant terrible (*Bob Kick the Mischievous Kid*), nos 510–511; 40 m

Les Illusions funambulesques (*Extraordinary Illusions*), nos 512–13; 50 m

L'Enchanteur Alcofribas (*Alcofribas, the Master Magician*), nos 514–16; 70 m

Jack et Jim (*Jack and Jim*), nos 517–19; 60 m

La Lanterne magique (*The Magic Lantern*), nos 520–5; 100 m

Le Rêve du maître de ballet (*The Ballet Master's Dream*), nos 525–6; 50 m

Faust aux enfers (*The Damnation of Faust*), nos 527–33; 145 m

1904

Le Bourreau turc (*The Terrible Turkish Executioner*), nos 534–5; 45 m

Au clair de la Lune ou Pierrot malheureux (*A Moonlight Serenade, or The Miser Punished*), nos 538–9; 55 m

Un prêté pour un rendu (Une bonne farce avec ma tête) (*Tit for Tat*), nos 540–1; 40 m

Un peu de feu S.V.P. (*Every Man His Own Cigar Lighter*), no. 545; 20 m

Le Coffre enchanté (*The Bewitched Trunk*), nos 547–9; 50 m

Les Apparitions fugitives (*Fugitive Apparitions*), nos 550–1; 40 m

Le Roi du maquillage (*Untamable Whiskers*), nos 552–3; 45 m

Le Rêve de l'horloger (*The Clockmaker's Dream*), nos 554–5; 50 m

Les Transmutations imperceptibles (*The Imperceptible Transmutations*), nos 556–7; 40 m

Un miracle sous l'Inquisition (*A Miracle Under the Inquisition*), nos 558–9; 45 m

Benvenuto Cellini ou Curieuse Évasion (*Benvenuto Cellini, or A Curious Evasion*), nos 560–1; 55 m

Damnation du docteur Faust (*Faust and Marguerite*), nos 562–74; 260 m

Le Thaumaturge chinois (*Tchin-Chao, the Chinese Conjurer*), nos 578–80; 60 m

Le Merveilleux Éventail vivant (*The Wonderful Living Fan*), nos 581–4; 90 m

Sorcellerie culinaire (*The Cook in Trouble*), nos 585–8; 85 m

La Planche du diable (*The Devilish Plank*), nos 589–90; 40 m

La Sirène (*The Mermaid*), nos 593–5; 70 m

Voyage à travers l'impossible (*The Impossible Voyage*), nos 641–59; 374 m

Le Juif errant (*The Wandering Jew*), nos 662–4; 60 m

La Cascade de feu (*The Firefall*), nos 665–7; 60 m

Détresse et charité (*L'Ange de Noël*) (*The Christmas Angel*), nos 669–77; 190 m

Les Cartes vivantes (*The Living Playing Cards*), nos 678–9; 50 m

1905

Le Diable noir (*The Black Imp*), nos 683–5; 70 m

Le Phénix ou le Coffret de cristal (*The Crystal Casket*), nos 686–9; 90 m

Le Menuet lilliputien (*The Lilliputian Minuet*), nos 690–2; 60 m

Le Banquet de Mesmer (*A Mesmerian Experiment*), nos 693–5; 60 m

Le Palais des mille et une nuits (*The Palace of the Arabian Nights*), nos 705–26; 440 m

La Chaise à porteurs enchantée (*The Enchanted Sedan Chair*), nos 738–9; 55 m

Le Raid Paris-Monte Carlo en deux heures (*The Adventurous Automobile Trip*), nos 740–9; 200 m

L'Ile de Calypso (*The Mysterious Island*), nos 750–2, 70 m

Un feu d'artifice improvisé (*Unexpected Fireworks*), nos 753–5; 60 m

La Légende de Rip Van Winckle (*Rip's Dream*), nos 756–75; 405 m

Le Tripot clandestin (*The Scheming Gambler's Paradise*), nos 784–5; 55 m

Le dirigeable fantastique ou le Cauchemar d'un inventeur (*The Inventor Crazybrains and His Wonderful Airship*), nos 786–8; 60 m

Une chute de cinq étages (*A Mix-up in the Gallery*), nos 789–90; 55 m

Jack le ramoneur (*The Chimney Sweep*), nos 791–806; 320 m

Le Maestro Do-Mi-Sol-Do (*Professor Do-mi-sol-do*), nos 808–9; 65 m

1906

La Cardeuse de matelas (*The Tramp and the Mattress Makers*), nos 818–20; 75 m

Les Affiches en goguette (*The Hilarious Posters*), nos 821–3; 60 m

Les Incendiaires (*Histoire d'un crime*) (*A Desperate Crime*), nos 824–37; 280 m

L'Anarchie chez Guignol (*Punch and Judy*), nos 838–9; 40 m

L'Hôtel des voyageurs de commerce (*A Roadside Inn*), nos 843–5; 75 m

Les Bulles de savon animées (*Soap Bubbles*), nos 846–8; 72 m

Les Quat'cents Farces du diable (*The Merry Frolics of Satan*), nos 849–70; 444 m

L'Alchimiste Parafaragaramus ou la Cornue infernale (*The Mysterious Retort*), nos 874–6; 60 m

La Fée Carabosse ou le Poignard fatal (*The Witch*), nos 877–87; 236 m

Robert Macaire et Bertrand (*Robert Macaire and Bertrand*), nos 888–905; 364 m

1907

La Douche d'eau bouillante (*Rogue's Tricks*), nos 909–11; 75 m

Deux Cents Milles sous les mers (*Under the Seas*), nos 912–24; 265 m

Le mariage de Victorine (*How Bridget's Lover Escaped*), nos 929–935, 142 m

Le Tunnel sous la Manche, ou le Cauchemear franco-anglais (*Tunnelling the English Channel*), nos 936–50; 305 m

Éclipse du Soleil en pleine Lune (*The Eclipse, or the Courtship of the Sun and the Moon*), nos 961–8; 170 m

Pauvre John ou les Aventures d'un buveur de whisky (*Sight-seeing Through Whiskey*), nos 1000–4; 110 m

La Colle universelle (Good Glue Sticks), nos 1005–9; 100 m

Satan en prison (Satan in Prison), nos 1010–13; 90 m

Ali Barboyou et Ali Bouf à l'huile (Delirium in a Studio), nos 1014–17; 90 m

Le Tambourin fantastique (The Knight of the Black Art), nos 1030–4; 115 m

Il y a un dieu pour les ivrognes (The Good Luck of a 'Souse'), nos 1044–9; 135 m

1908

Le Génie du feu (The Genii of Fire), nos 1069–72; 95 m

Why that actor was late, nos 1073–80; 175 m

Le Rêve d'un fumeur d'opium (The Dream of an Opium Fiend), nos 1081–5; 105 m

La Photographie électrique à distance (Long Distance Wireless Photography), nos 1091–5; 115 m

Salon de coiffure (In the Barber Shop), nos 1102–3; 53 m

Le Nouveau Seigneur du village (The New Lord of the Village), nos 1132–45; 297 m

L'Avare (The Miser), nos 1146–58; 270 m

Le conseil du pipelet ou Un tour à la foire (Up-to-Date Clothes Cleaning), nos 1159–65; 143 m

Lully ou le Violon brisé (The Broken Violin), nos 1176–85; 208 m

The Woes of Roller Skaters, nos 1227–32; 140 m

Love and Molasse (His First Job), nos 1246–9; 95 m

The Mischances of a Photographer, nos 1250–2; 65 m

Le Fakir de Singapour (The Indian Sorcerer), nos 1253–7; 105 m

A Tricky Painter's Fate, nos 1266–8; 75 m

French interpreter policeman, nos 1288–93; 138 m

Anaïc ou le Balafré (Anaic, or The One with the Gash), nos 1301–9; 192 m

Pour l'étoile S.V.P. (Spare Change for the Star, Please), nos 1310–13; 77 m

Conte de la grand-mère et Rêve de l'enfant ou Au Pays des jouets (Grandmother's Story), nos 1314–25, 243 m

Hallucinations pharmaceutiques ou le Truc du potard (Pharmaceutical Hallucinations), nos 1416–28; 260 m

La Bonne Bergère et la Mauvaise Princesse (The Good Shepherdess and the Evil Princess), nos 1429–41; 280 m

1909

Hydrothérapie fantastique (*The Doctor's Secret*), nos 1476–85; 24 m
Le Locataire diabolique (*The Diabolic Tenant*), nos 1495–1501; 120 m
Les Illusions fantaisistes (*Whimsical Illusions*), nos 1508–12; 100 m

1911

Les Hallucinations du baron de Münchausen (*Baron Münchausen's Dream*), nos 1536–47; 235 m

1912

(Films made for Pathé)
A la conquête du Pôle (*The Conquest of the Pole*); 650 m
Cendrillon ou la Pantoufle merveilleuse (*Cinderella or the Glass Slipper*); 615 m
Le Chevalier des neiges (*The Knight of the Snows*); 400 m

Select bibliography

Works on Méliès

Bessy, M. and Duca, L., *Georges Méliès, Mage*, Paris, Jean-Jacques Pauvert, 1961. One of the earliest books devoted to Méliès. Consisting of biography, synopses of selected films and an autobiographical text written by Méliès in the third person, this book is a good source of photos and illustrations. Because it was written when there were many more gaps in Méliès's *oeuvre*, there are several inaccuracies: for example, a photographic caption misidentifies Edison's *Dream of a Rarebit Fiend* as a 'film inconnu de Méliès' (213), and a still photo from *La Lanterne magique* is identified as *Le Paradis des jouets* (162).

Frazer, John, *Artificially Arranged Scenes*, Boston, MA, G. K. Hall and Co., 1979. This is the most systematic and comprehensive study of Méliès's films, which situates them in their historical and artistic context and provides detailed plot summaries and production notes for all of the films known to be extant at the time of the book's publication. Despite the occasional outdated piece of information that has been superceded by more recent scholarship (to which I have drawn attention at appropriate points throughout this study), this book remains the single most useful resource for students of Méliès.

Hammond, Paul, *Marvellous Méliès*, London, Gordon Fraser, 1974. An overview of Méliès's career, with some discussion of themes and production techniques used in the films. Contains a number of helpful photographs, with a few pages devoted to the film career of Méliès's brother Gaston.

Jenn, Pierre, *Georges Méliès Cinéaste*, Paris, Editions Albatros, 1984. A short study written primarily for the purpose of demonstrating (with the aid of several diagrams) that, based on two episodes of *L'Affaire Dreyfus* (*Attentat contre maître Labori* and *Bagarre entre journalistes*), Méliès was capable of using unequivocally cinematic, as opposed to theatrical, techniques.

Malthête, Jacques, *Méliès, Images et Illusions,* Paris, Exporégie, 1996. A compendium of biographical and technical information, filled with handsomely reproduced colour illustrations and photographs, by the researcher who has made perhaps the most extensive contribution to Méliès scholarship to date. Malthête specializes in the technical aspects of Méliès's production practices. Also contains original poetry and drawings by Méliès. Many of the essays contained in this volume have been published previously in journals.

Malthête, Jacques and Marie, Michel (eds), *Méliès, l'illusionniste fin de siècle?*, actes du colloque Méliès 1996, Paris, Presses de la Sorbonne nouvelle, 1998. A very mixed collection of essays, with many of the contributions using Méliès's work as little more than a pretext for discussing other subjects.

Malthête-Méliès, Madeleine, *Méliès l'enchanteur*, Paris, Hachette, 1973 (reprinted in 1995 by Ramsey, Paris). A memoir written by Méliès's granddaughter. A useful resource, although it devotes rather a lot of space to Méliès's romantic life.

Malthête-Méliès, Madeleine (ed.), *Méliès et la naissance du spectacle cinématographe*, (Paris), Klincksieck, 1984. A collection of papers presented at a meeting of the Société des amis de Méliès. Each paper is on a different, fairly specific topic.

Malthête-Méliès, Madeleine *et al.*, *Essai de Reconstitution du Catalogue Français de la Star-Film suivi d'une Analyse Catalographique des Films de Georges Méliès recensés en France*, (Paris), Centre National de la Cinématographie, 1981. The definitive catalogue of Méliès's extant French films, with locations, detailed descriptions and English and American titles when applicable. An invaluable research tool. Supplemented by the *Analyse descriptive des films de Georges Méliès rassemblés entre 1981 et 1996 par la cinémathèque Méliès* .

Méliès, Gaston, *Le Voyage autour du monde de la G. Méliès Manufacturing Company*, Paris, Association 'Les Amis de Georges Méliès', 1988. The most comprehensive (although by no means exhaustive) source of information about the film-making career of Méliès's brother, this book contains letters written by Gaston to his son Paul, who directed the New York office of Star-Film while Gaston was making films in the United States and the South Pacific.

Robinson, David, *Georges Méliès, Father of Film Fantasy*, London, Museum of the Moving Image, 1993. A brief overview of Méliès's life and work, this booklet was produced in conjunction with an exhibition on Méliès at the Museum of the Moving Image in London. Contains many photographs, and some original bio-graphical research.

Sadoul, Georges, *Georges Méliès*, Paris, Seghers, 1970 (first printed in 1961). An early classic in the field, this study of Méliès's work has fared better than other scholarship produced in the same period, and remains an important resource. Also reprints texts written by Méliès himself.

Sadoul, Georges (ed.), Special Supplement to *Sight and Sound*, Index series no. 11, 'An Index to the Creative Work of Georges Méliès [1896-1912]', August 1947. Synopses of the films taken from the English Star-Film catalogue, written by Méliès himself.

General works on early French cinema

Abel, R., *The Ciné Goes to Town*, updated and expanded edition, Berkeley, University of California Press, 1998. An invaluable study of early French cinema written by a world authority. Although the discussions of Méliès are not always based on the most current research, this wide-ranging and illuminating book should nonetheless be required reading for any student or scholar of early French film.

Deslandes, J., *Le Boulevard du cinéma à l'époque de Georges Méliès*, Paris, Editions du Cerf, 1963. An early classic in the field of Méliès studies which, although surpassed by more recent scholarship, still offers much useful information.

Elsaesser, T. (ed.), *Early Cinema: Space, Frame, Narrative* , London, BFI, 1990. The essays in this book engage in many of the important critical debates surrounding Méliès's contribution to early cinema. A very valuable resource.

Fell, John L. (ed.), *Film Before Griffith*, Berkeley, University of California Press, 1983. A useful collection of essays about early film history, including pieces on the development of production, distribution and exhibition practices in France, the USA and Britain, and formal analysis of structural aspects of early cinema.

Gili, J. A. *et al.* (eds). *Les vingt premières années du cinéma français*, Paris, Presses de la Sorbonne Nouvelle, 1995. Méliès's work is discussed in several of the articles devoted to the cinema of attractions, notably those by Charles Musser and Tom Gunning.

Jeanne, René, *Cinéma 1900*, Paris, Flammarion, 1965. The first few chapters of this book are devoted to Méliès, situating his career in the context of the fledgling cultural phenomenon of cinema.

Mitry, J., *Histoire du cinéma, volume I (1895–1914)*, Paris, Editions universitaires, 1968. One of the most respected film histories, this volume contains some discussion of Méliès.

Usai, Paoli Cherchi, *Burning Passions: An Introduction to the Study of Silent Cinema*, London, British Film Institute, 1994. Not limited to French cinema, but an important resource for film scholars, containing technical information and advice about working in early film archives.

Williams, Alan, *Republic of Images: A History of French Film-making*, Cambridge, MA, Harvard University Press, 1992. A lively, single-volume history of French cinema, which engages seriously with some of Méliès's films.

Index

Note: 'n' after a page reference indicates a note number on that page.